ONE AGAINST THE STORM

ONE AGAINST THE STORM

by **Stanley C. Mann**

An original publication of Quest Publications
This work has never before appeared in book form

Quest Publishing, Inc.
Chicago, Illinois

ISBN 0-938662-00-7

Library of Congress Catalog Card Number 80-54238

© Copyright Stanley C. Mann 1980
P.O. Box 27317, Salt Lake City, Utah 84127

All rights reserved. No part of this book may be
reproduced in any form or by any
mechanical means, including mimeograph and
copy machines; without permission in
writing from the publisher

Printed in the United States of America

*To single parents
adoptive parents and
natural parents
everywhere*

Design by Freeman & Assoc.
Illustration by Harold T. Kilbourn

Author's Note

I decided to write this book on January 4, 1979, one week after my niece's death, when I went to her home in Denver, Colorado, to pack up her personal belongings and ready the house for sale. I was prepared for a traumatic experience. What I found was tangible, overwhelming evidence of her love and concern for little David, her adopted son. I shall never forget the three days I spent in Joan's home.

Immediately after this I knew that I had to compile a record of the events of her life for her "beloved David" so that the child, growing up without his mother, would have insight into her personality and character. She loved him so dearly. Her love simply had to count for something!

Joan's life had been plagued with unbelievable difficulties, but her death—and the aftermath—was bombarded with such bizarre and incredible circumstances as to bogle the human mind. Forces emerged to obliterate her human rights, to assassinate her character, and to destroy everything she had planned and worked for all of her adult life. Her story had to be told.

ONE AGAINST THE STORM is true. The people are real, their names unchanged. The documented incidents are examples of love, hate, greed, betrayal, discrimination, revenge that extends beyond the grave, legal chicanery, brutality, and perjury, judicial incompetence and dishonesty.

This book is an attempt to honor a promise to my dead niece. I took an oath that if I could not fulfill requests in her will and trust—and the courts have frustrated me at every turn in these matters—I would make every effort to locate her adopted son's natural parents in the hope that they might have married each other, or that one of them might recognize David's need and step forward to rescue the boy.

As executor of Joan's estate, I live in a nightmare, trying

to fulfill a simple commitment of love which has evolved into a series of nightmares. My family has received obscene phone calls, my life has been threatened and our way of life seriously disrupted because of my involvement in this situation. To date, I have spent thousands of hours and dollars fighting court battles in three states, trying to carry out terms specifically stated in Joan's last will and testament.

As a high-ranking executive with such firms as Lanvin-Charles of the Ritz, Helene Curtis Industries and Mars Incorporated, I have lived in many parts of this country and become acquainted with diverse life styles and mores. But never did I even suspect the degree of infamy and manipulation I've uncovered in this case. The story is unbelievable but true. I have documented every fact, every word, every action.

The professional people involved in this story are recognized in legal, judicial, political and religious circles; nonetheless they have lied, perjured, and subverted justice for personal gain. The victims?...Joan and David. God help you if you're dead—or a helpless child!

Many people have given me ideas, information, support and encouragement in the preparation and revisions of the manuscript for this book. In ordinary circumstances, common practice would dictate that the author would accord appropriate credits to those who furnished such assistance. However, in view of the nature of this book, and the startling facts that it lays bare, I decline to attribute credits to particular people, and thus needlessly draw them into the fray. Because, in all candor, this book is, and must be, mine. And mine alone!!

While many have realized that the account must be told, I am totally and exclusively responsible for the telling. No one, except me, is responsible for deciding to publish the volumes, and to reveal the astonishing and squalid details of a system of "justice" that makes a mockery of our present society.

Stanley C. Mann

Foreword

Discrimination and bigotry are not a thing of the past in the United States. Today the plight of the single woman raising a child alone is often a heart-breaking story of emotional, financial, religious and social turmoil. Yet my niece Joan and her son David had a unique relationship in their brief time together, despite the acts of lunacy and vengeance wreaked upon them by others.

Because of a demoralizing marriage and a devastating divorce, Joan had serious problems. She couldn't accept the fact that her ex-husband was an inveterate liar, gambler, and womanizer, but the facts were all there. Her mind had pointed this out on too many occasions for there to be any doubt.

She had provided financial resources for this man, several lovely homes, a stable income, automobiles, and other material possessions, to say nothing of cash, but he had spurned her in favor of liasons with other women. Childless after ten years of marriage, they had finally adopted a baby boy, a beautiful, healthy fellow—but the new father promptly abandoned both mother and child when the baby was only nine months old, on the very day the adoption became legal! He had already moved in with another woman.

Now that Joan is dead, this man swears devotion to the child. And the courts support him, even though he is an admitted felon who has been shot three times critically by an unknown assailant, is in debt at every turn in several states—and keeps the boy tranquilized!

Before Joan died, she made extensive plans to protect David from this man. I, her uncle, was named the administrator of her estate and the child's guardian; and although I did not know the details of her plans until after her death, I was fully aware of her fears and her distrust of her former husband. She did not want him to even touch the boy!

Neither did she want to live! She died in an airplane accident in December, 1978, but she had a premonition of death even before that last flight. As early as the previous January she had written in a letter that she didn't care to live much longer, and in March of 1978 she asked me, "Uncle Stan, do you think I could be buried in the family plot?" In the fall of the same year she went out to the sexton's office in the cemetery at Bountiful, Utah, and wrote her name on the plot map. And in November, just two months before the fatal crash, she told a fellow flight attendant, "I have the feeling that the Lord won't make me suffer much longer."

Joan often spent time with our family. Christmases and other holidays often found her adding to our family fun. She and David were a part of us. We loved them as we loved our own children. We reveled in their successes; we worried about their sorrows; we shared in their financial burdens, but most of all, we loved them.

The Christmas of 1978 was our last shared holiday. I'm grateful we could not see into the future at that time. At least we shared one more warm, loving family celebration before both she and David were snatched from us.

What kind of person was this niece of mine, this woman thirty-six years old, a quality human being at the height of her career as a top flight attendant? In spite of her successes, sometimes she seemed like a little girl, unsure of herself. Shaken by a demeaning divorce and plagued all of her life by people who took advantage of her gentle disposition, Joan knew only one thing: that she wanted the best that life had to offer for her adopted son to whom she was devoted.

After her death was confirmed, as I sat there holding the boy, I promised myself—and her—that I would do everything I could to insure a good life for David. I would give him a loving home, I would care for him physically and guard the trust fund Joan had set up for his welfare.

Despite my vow, during the next few days the law tore David out of my arms and placed him in a home environment surrounded by complete strangers, a home where he is under tranquilization, where his needs are not only ignored, but where there are negative factors so adverse as to render the boy's future competency in jeopardy. And now even his trust is in danger!

Dear Joan, I have failed you.

Tears stream down my face unchecked as I remember the vigor of David's healthy body when I held him those last hours. "I love you, Grandpa, but I don't want to live in your house forever. I want Mama back. I want to go home and live with my Mama."

But his Mama was dead. He could not go home again. Ever.

I wiped the tears away impatiently and made my dead niece another promise. As God is my witness, Joan, I will not let them take that boy's money. And if there is any way I can find David's natural parents, I will do it! Whatever it requires —court cases, money, even imprisonment—no matter what the cost, I'll stand by your last wishes.

You can count on Uncle Stan, come hell or high water.

ONE AGAINST THE STORM

Christmas of 1978	1
A Senseless Tragedy	13
The Disrespect of Last Respects	30
First the Mother, Then the Son	41
Last Child of the Third Family	61
Enter: Wheeler the Dealer	67
Civilian Life with a Con-Artist	74
A Heavy Family Man	81
David, Child of Love	89
The Great Cover-Up	96
The Manipulator Revealed	101
Sylvi—(Sunn) Classic Mother Figure	109
A Rock in Time of Trouble	117
Shauna, The Family Adversary	122
C. W.—Victim of His Own Child's Greed	132
The Source of It All	138
The Stigma of Divorce	147
A.D.: The Fight Begins	156
Legal Chicanery	162
More Chicanery	175
Piety and Perversion	183
Birds of a Feather	188
And So It Stands	195
Afterword	208

Christmas of 1978

Joan often spent holidays with our family and the Christmas of 1978 was no exception. She and David arrived on December 18th, carrying all the presents they could hold. We were a big family and Joan continued to shop and work on gifts right up to the deadline of Christmas Eve. In fact, she was sewing a special stocking on Christmas Day.
    And what a stocking it was, a sequin-crusted Santa, holding a colorful felt train engine trimmed in gold braid with its track running around old Santa's feet. Each tiny tie on the railroad track was hand-sewn. Several elves with embroidered faces and hair operated various switches, lights, and tunnels. The scene was timed by a cuckoo clock with hands that moved, and the whole stocking was topped by an ornate "DAVID" in gold.
    We were especially pleased to see her this year because she seemed more optimistic, more hopeful than she had been for some time, but we were also disappointed when she told us, right after her arrival, that she had "sold" fourteen days

of her vacation because she needed the money. She was to fly out the next day and again on the 28th. Mark had not paid support money in almost two years.

We drove her to the airport, saw her off on her scheduled flight and took David home with us. What a bright, loving little boy he was. We had a special game that we played. He would throw his arms around my neck and say, "I love you, Grandpa!—Clear over to my place and back, over to the ocean and to the mountains and clear up to the sky and back!" We tried to out do him by telling him how much *we* loved *him*, but I think it was a toss-up.

Earlier Joan had asked how we would feel if David called us "Grandpa" and "Grandma." She said, "You have always seemed so much more than an uncle to me and we have spent so much time in your home that I wonder if I could ask you and Aunt Louise to play that role for David? I want him to have the feeling of belonging to a family." Her own parents were both dead by this time, and Mark's folks never acknowledged David because he was adopted.

I quickly agreed to her request. He seemed like a grandson to us, anyway.

We had a wonderful Christmas with all the trimmings and the family at home, but on the night of the 27th we took Joan to the airport to return to Denver. She had to exchange a number of gifts she had purchased for David's Christmas as they were too small—how he had grown since she purchased them some months ago! His usual size four clothes would have to be exchanged for a larger size!

After working on the 28th Joan planned to return to Salt Lake to spend another five days with us. We were all looking forward to that when we put her on her flight and kept David with us. He would liven up the remainder of the holiday.

During the day on December 28th, David went to the office with Louise and me. He played in the meeting room all morning, then after lunch and a nap, he came into my office to see if he could help me work. I gave him some small jobs to do and paid him five nickels. The whole office staff was amazed at how well he played with his toys and how content he seemed. He carried the mail from one office to another and put it into file boxes. He was so tickled that he could help Grandma and Grandpa—and earn money, too! Our youngest son and our daughter came down to the office and the two of them plus Louise and David and I went out to dinner. Thrilled with his five nickels, David offered to pay the check!

We arrived home about 7 P.M. I told David if he would take his bath and get ready for bed, he could stay up and go to the airport to pick up his mother. I had to compromise by bathing with him, since the bath involved a shampoo which he hated. I didn't mind, however, because David's monologue and comparisons of our body parts would have rated with the best quips Bob Hope ever delivered.

It was a little after eight o'clock—we had forty-five minutes left before we were to leave to get Joan—when our son Brett walked into the bedroom to tell us that a report of an airplane crash in Portland had just flashed on TV.

"A small plane or an airliner?" I asked, my heart in my throat.

He didn't know. He just caught the end of it. I turned our TV on to another channel, but Brett came in again with another report. It was a United Airlines DC-8 Jetliner that had gone down. The news stunned all of us. I decided to call United in Denver. The receptionist came on and I explained that I was greatly concerned because my niece had been on a flight going into Portland. Was it her plane that had crashed?

She asked me to wait a moment while she referred me to someone else. Soon another woman took the line, and I repeated what I had told the first girl and asked her if the plane that went down had a Denver-based crew. She said she would check it out and call me back, but she thought the crew originated in New York. I told her Joan's name and said she was a stewardess flying to Portland that day. She would check on Joan's status and let me know as soon as possible.

We waited about thirty minutes without hearing anything. It was about time to leave for the airport when the phone rang. My daughter answered. We stopped in our tracks, and Micalle called, "Daddy, they want a Mr. Moon." That sounded too close to Mann for me to ignore. I asked her to inquire if they meant Mr. Mann. Was it United Airlines calling? It was.

I took the phone. Was this call in reference to Joan Wheeler? The voice said, "Let me refer you to my supervisor, sir."

I waited impatiently and finally I heard, "This is Marilyn McArthur, United Airlines Personnel Department. May I help you?"

I explained my relationship to Joan and Mrs. McArthur offered to pull Joan's file. After referring to it, she said, "Yes, it was Mr. Mann we were asking for. Joan has listed your name on her file as the individual to contact in case of emergency. The instructions are that we give no information out to anyone else under any circumstances." She then told me that there had been a crash in Portland.

"Yes, I know," I said. "Was Joan hurt?"

She didn't know, but all relatives were being notified. "May I call you later tonight if we get some kind of information?"

I said we would be waiting for her call. I hung up the phone and told Louise what she had already heard. I told little David that his mother's flight had been delayed and that he should go to bed. The rest of us sat stunned. About this time another news flash confirmed the fact that there had been fatalities, but they didn't have many details.

We prepared for a long night. A short time later the phone rang. I snatched it up only to learn from Marilyn McArthur that there were some survivors but she did not know how many. She would call back when she had more information.

Thirty minutes later she called again. "Nothing is confirmed, but it doesn't look good for Joan. Our indications are that Joan might have been one of the fatalities."

At this point I resigned myself that Joan was gone. A feeling told me she was dead. But less than an hour later United called and informed me that my niece Joan Wheeler had not been on that flight. When I asked her where Joan was, she said, "Why, sir, how would I know?" and my heart fell again. "My niece is a stewardess," I told her, "and if she wasn't on that flight, she should have called in sick."

There was dead silence on the line. Then the voice said, "Let me connect you with my supervisor." After a long pause, the supervisor apologized. "I am sorry, sir. We didn't know that your niece was a stewardess. We only checked the passenger list. I will check further and call you back."

I decided we had better contact Joan's sister, Gail. I told her that Joan's flight had gone down, but we should wait for confirmation before calling her brother Charley.

About one o'clock in the morning the bad news was confirmed. Marilyn called. Joan was indeed one of the fatalities. If we wanted to fly to Portland to identify her remains, United would handle the arrangements. I told her there would be no need for this as long as positive identification had been made. She confirmed that it had.

She said their Salt Lake manager would be in touch with me first thing in the morning and she asked for my office address. No one could have been more accommodating than the people at United Airlines. Mrs. McArthur kept me informed and rendered valuable aid to us through the whole tragedy. The next morning Mr. Norman Rasmussen met me at my office with a benefits insurance check for one thousand dollars for immediate expenses. He expressed the airline's sympathy.

Now we had to face the family. Because of past animosities this was going to be difficult. I called Gail and told her the worst had been confirmed. I asked her if she wanted to call Charley and Virginia Kohtz, a sort of half-sister who had been close to Joan, or if she wanted me to call them. She agreed to do the telephoning, but asked if she should call Joan's sister Shauna, too. Joan's specific wish, in case anything happened to her, was that neither Mark, her ex-husband, nor Shauna were to be notified. It was a reasonable request in view of all the troubles they heaped upon her shoulders while she was still alive. I told Gail I would honor that request.

In my safe was Joan's original will along with a letter which she had given me the previous spring, and I told Gail I thought the letter contained a list of personal things and how they should be disposed. I would call Joan's lawyer, Byron Fisher, and we could go over together around ten o'clock.

The next morning I made the appointment and waited for Gail. When she hadn't arrived by 11 o'clock, I telephoned the lawyer and postponed the appointment until noon. Then at noon I had to postpone until 2 P.M. hoping that Gail would arrive. She finally came to my office about one o'clock, with her husband, Glenn. I expressed my concern that something might have happened to them, but they overlooked my remark.

Glenn said he felt now was the time to heal past wounds, but we were late for our appointment so I urged them to come to the lawyer's with me and we would talk about Mark and Shauna later. As I picked up Joan's will and her letter, I told my wife that I thought Gail and Glenn had been consulting with Shauna and her husband Dave, and that was the reason they were delayed that morning.

I held the letter in my hands with no foreboding as to its contents, but fortunately I had the insight to refuse to open it until it was in the hands of the attorney. It was sealed with

Joan's signature and I wanted the lawyer to witness that it had not been tampered with.

The lawyer read the will, testifying first that he had met with Joan, prepared the document himself, and knew that it contained her expressed wishes. I could see that some of the provisions in the will were a surprise to Gail and Glenn. Parts of the will read:

> (b) DISTRIBUTION. This trust shall continue until there shall be no child of mine living who is under the age of twenty-five (25) years, when Trustee shall distribute all of the remainder of the trust properties in equal shares to my living children and upon the principle of representation to the living descendants of those of my children who may be deceased.
>
> In the event my spouse, my children and all of my children's descendants predecease the date of final distribution provided above, the Trustee shall distribute all of the remainder of the trust properties as follows:
>
> $5,000 each to Gail H. Taylor, Charles M. Hartley and Virginia H. Kohtz, all of the rest, residue and remainder to Stanley C. Mann.
>
> In the event that the guardian of my minor children legally adopt them, then the trust provided herein for the care of my minor children shall terminate and shall be distributed entirely to the guardians to be used as they deem proper for the use and benefit of the guardians and their entire family.
>
> VII. APPOINTMENT OF FIDUCIARIES. I appoint Stanley C. Mann, to be Executor of my will, to serve without bond. In the event Stanley C. Mann dies, declines to act or otherwise does not serve as Executor of my will, I appoint Gail H. Taylor to serve as Executrix of my will, to serve without bond.

I appoint Stanley C. Mann to be Trustee of the trust created by my will. In the event Stanley C. Mann dies, declines to act or otherwise does not serve as trustee, I appoint Gail H. Taylor to be Trustee of the trust created by my will. No Trustee appointed hereunder need give bond.

I appoint Stanley C. Mann and Louise S. Mann as joint guardians of my minor children and of the estate of any minor child of mine, to serve without bond.

But their surprise at the will was nothing compared to the surprise they—and I—had in store when the letter was opened. Gail was asked to identify Joan's handwriting and the letter was unsealed. It was addressed to "Uncle Stan and Aunt Louise" and, according to the date, it had been written two months before she handed it to me to keep. I had expected a list of her belongings and their disposition. Joan had asked me if I wanted to know how she was distributing her things, but I told her that I specifically did *not* want to know.

The letter was a blockbuster.

Uncle Stan and Aunt Louise, 1-23-78

I want you both to make all the arrangements to take care of my remains. I have no desire to live long—death is a real relief. Please bury me in Bountiful on my Grandfather Mann's plot. I want no autopsy, a closed casket and graveside services.

Please love and care for my beloved little David—try to keep that horrible Mark away from him. I hope you will be able to adopt and seal him. The one request I have concerning his upbringing is to really try to encourage him to go on a mission—always talk to him in terms of *when* he goes on his mission.

As for the poodle and cats, they are getting old and it would probably be best to put them to sleep.

Follow the will/trust. I want neither Shauna, Gail, or

Charley in my home—they never bothered about me before so I don't want them around now.

Thank you for all your concern and just caring—

Love, Joan

After the letter was read, silence filled the room. Finally Byron broke it by saying, "Well, that was one of the things about Joan. She was very direct. You always knew where you stood with her. She left no doubt about her feelings."

I was as stunned as anyone else. We started back to my office. I told Gail that I would appreciate her helping with arrangements for the funeral, that although it was not the usual type of service for members of our faith, I would honor Joan's wishes since she had been very definite.

I tried to soften the blow of Joan's letter by telling Gail and Glenn that I thought Joan did not feel the same way as she had when the letter was written, just shortly after the death of her father, eleven months before. There had been so much turmoil over the old man's will that family feelings were strong, and Joan had been hurt to the quick over Shauna's treatment of her father and Gail's "peace-at-any-cost" attitude. Joan had felt deserted and alone.

When we sat down in the office, Glenn asked if I didn't think we should call Mark. Why, I wondered. I was surprised he would suggest such a move.

"No," I stated flatly. "I don't think we should call Mark."

He retaliated by asking if I really intended to follow Joan's instructions concerning the funeral. I certainly did. Then Glenn interjected, "Don't you think it is time for Joan's immediate family to take over and make arrangements?"

I looked him in the eye for a moment, then asked, "And who is Joan's immediate family?" Without waiting for an answer I told him that, according to the terms of the will and her instructions in the letter, Joan asked me to carry out the decisions that she herself made. She did not leave these matters for the immediate family—or even me—to make. She made them herself. I asked Glenn if he had a will. He replied that he had. "Do you expect those wishes to be carried out?" I inquired. He was silent.

I recalled Joan's exact words: "Uncle Stan, if you never do anything else for me, please do this."

At that time I was reluctant to administer her will, but she said she could not trust anyone else to carry out her wishes. I was taken back by the turn of events, but Joan had apparently anticipated these very reactions. I had the feeling that Gail was torn between the wishes of her sister and the position her husband had taken. I looked at Gail and told her that I intended to carry out Joan's expressed wishes and I would like her to help me make arrangements in the manner that Joan requested. This she did.

That afternoon, the 29th, Marilyn McArthur called to let me know that Mark Wheeler had telephoned the airlines for an official notice of Joan's fatality. They told him they were not authorized to give him this; according to Joan's instructions, they were to release information only to Stanley C. Mann. Mark, of course, had my address and telephone number, but he had made no effort to get hold of me or to learn David's whereabouts. He was only interested in an official acknowledgement of Joan's death.

Later that afternoon Marilyn called again. "Mr. Mann, United Airlines just received the funniest call from a Mrs. Henrietta Young, who identified herself as Shauna Young's mother-in-law. She asked all kinds of questions of a legal nature—questions we have never heard before from a family survivor."

I asked her what information they gave her, but she answered, "We gave her no information. We referred her to you."

A short time later I received a telephone call from a coroner in Portland. He had received a call from this same

Mrs. Young. She asked in great detail about the body. If the body had been taken to a hospital in Portland, when would it arrive in Salt Lake City, and would the personal effects accompany the body? He told her he was not authorized to release any information.

I couldn't believe that Henrietta would let herself be used this way, but I knew who was behind those calls—Shauna's husband, Dave. My brother Charley had had all kinds of difficulties administering Joan's mother's estate because of Dave's meddling. I told Byron Fisher under no circumstances to discuss Joan's estate with Dave Young.

At 2 A.M. Saturday morning, Mark called me. He was irate. "Where is my boy?" he shouted into the phone. I tried to wake up. I told him I didn't know he cared. He had made no effort to contact David previously—or to support him. He ignored me. "I am coming to get him," he roared.

"Settle down, Mark," I advised him. "That kind of attitude will not solve any problems." He asked again where the boy was, and I said he was with family and was well cared for.

"You have no right to him!" Mark hollered into the receiver. Then he hung up.

When morning finally came, I figured that if I informed Mark of the terms of Joan's will, that she had arranged for me to raise the boy and that a trust had been set up—there was no way he could get any money—it would solve the problem. I tried to telephone him long distance, but information said they had no Mark Wheeler listed in Northridge, California. Then I called my sister in Rupert, Idaho, for Mark's mother's number. But when I called, his mother refused to give me Mark's number. She said, however, that she would pass on the message that I wanted to speak with him.

About an hour-and-a-half later he called me. He started laying on the charm, saying how pleased he was that I had been named executor of Joan's estate. I told him outright that

I would like to have the lawyer call him to tell him the provisions of Joan's will, the plans she had made for David and the terms of the trust. I thought that if he heard directly from the lawyer, he would be forced to accept it. He refused to give me his telephone number, but he said he would call the lawyer himself. He added that he wanted to come to Joan's funeral. How did I think the family would receive him?

"I don't think that would be a good idea, Mark," I told him. "Joan's wish was that you not be present."

He ignored me and asked again how I felt the family would treat him. I assured him that we would not be rude to him, but he could hardly expect us to be friendly under the circumstances. All of the family knew how he had behaved before, during, and after the divorce. We were all greatly relieved when he did not show up for the service.

Byron informed me that Mark had called and he had set him straight. This relieved me. Mark soon called me back and said he thought he understood things clearly. "I won't cause any trouble, but I really haven't decided what to do at this point."

I fully believed that Mark would let the matter drop. He would have, too, if only both of his brothers-in-law, Wayne Wadsworth and David Young, had not advised him. They thought there was a good chance that if he gained custody of the boy, he could still get control of the trust money.

I didn't know it at the time, but things were just beginning to gain momentum. It would be a long fight, and the issues would be more complicated than anything I had ever encountered in my life—or even heard of, for that matter.

But for now, we had a funeral to get through. We tried to lay aside the confusion of the relationships at this point and show proper respect for our dear Joan. In effect, we had lost a daughter. And, although we had no premonition of it, we were also about to lose little David. As complicated as things seemed, they were simple compared to the legal and emotional turmoil we would soon find ourselves embroiled in.

A Senseless Tragedy

The crash that claimed the life of David's mother, Joan Wheeler, occurred on Thursday, December 28, 1978, just three days after we celebrated our last Christmas together. Although the lives of ten people were lost in that fatal crash, Joan's efforts accounted for the safety of many others. A newspaper account of the wreck stated "Chief Stewardess Joan Wheeler, in charge of preparing the cabin for the crash, was largely responsible for the survival of most of the passengers, McBroom (the pilot) said, and added that 'She was a damn good stewardess.'"

But Joan was dead. Her body, situated near the front of the cabin, which bore the brunt of greatest impact on contact, was found ruptured in ten or more places. Her uniform was saturated with blood. It had to be destroyed, so massive were her wounds. Her death was instantaneous. But she had done her job well.

One can only imagine the unmitigated horror Joan had to contend with as passengers faced the unknown when the big jetliner faltered through the cold evening air, only minutes from touchdown at Portland International Airport. First, two spine-chilling jolts rocked the aircraft. Passengers turned to each other in bewilderment, their faces ashen, their hearts beating wildly. Yet the plane's engines continued to whirr. Perhaps it was only an air pocket, one gentleman reassured those around him.

Another newspaper reported: Soon the pilot's intercom crackled on. "er, ladies and gentlemen, this is your captain speaking. That loud noise you heard a few minutes ago was the landing gear going down. One of the lights up here in the cockpit indicates that we do have an abnormal situation on our hands. We're going to stay at about five thousand feet and circle the city for about 20 minutes while we check it out. There's...er, no cause for alarm."

—No cause for alarm?—An abnormal situation? Minds desperately wrestle with this information. How should they prepare? How serious was it? With terror they light on the final question: will they all die?

Let it be a dream, mothers pray, or if it isn't a dream, please preserve my children. Oh, please, let it be some monstrous nightmare.

Joan goes into the cockpit, then comes out, her face drained of all color, her expression stunned. The pilot clicks back on the intercom. "Ladies and gentlemen, we are still checking out the landing gear. In the meantime we are going to have the stewardesses give you an explanation of emergency procedures...er, just in case. We have an excellent crew and an off-duty captain who will take care of things in the cabin. Simply do as they say. They are fully trained to handle an emergency landing should it occur."

And with this announcement Senior Flight Attendant Joan Wheeler takes over. "Ladies and gentlemen, we will be handing out pillows and blankets. Will you please take out the safety information card from the seat pocket in front and familiarize yourself with the safety procedures and emergency exits of this aircraft?"

In fifteen years Joan has never faced an emergency landing, but she is well trained. She instills confidence and trust in her passengers.

Stewardesses file up and down the aisles, distributing pillows and blankets and giving out instructions and encouragement. No one is more active than Joan. The safety of passengers and crew is her responsibility and she handles it well.

When everyone has removed their glasses, jewelry and shoes, children and grown-ups alike are strapped into their seats. In the galley, Nancy King, another stewardess, helps Joan with preparations.

Suddenly Nancy gasps, "Look, Joan!" Her eyes are glued to the small window in the supply door. She screams. "I can see street lights—and TREES!"

There has been no announcement of a landing from the captain but both of the girls rush toward their jump seats. Nancy's seat is near at hand, but the last she sees of Joan, she is heading toward the cockpit, half-way up the aisle, when the lights go out. Joan apparently reaches her seat, but does not strap herself in. Her voice is heard trying to make contact with the cockpit. "There's no one there," she states. The power is out and they are about to crash.

The plane is rocked by a horrifying bump, then another. Seat belts bite into stomachs as the force of the deccelerating plane throws everyone forward. Tearing metal, splintering wood, screams, groans and prayers fill the air. Then an eerie silence, soon broken by cries. "Get to the exits! Get to the exits! Go! Go! Go!" None of the commands are Joan's.

As the smoke settled and screams turned to moans, Nancy finished placing an injured man on a stretcher as stewardess Sandy Bass said to her, "I've found Joan."

Nancy looked up from the passenger she was comforting. "Where?" she questioned, dreading the answer. She started to turn around. Sandy stopped her abruptly. "Right behind you—but don't look. She's...she's dead."

Joan lay in the middle of a pile of debris where the demolished bulkhead had separated from the rest of the aircraft on impact. She was still, thrown out of the plane into the woods of Oregon only six miles from the Portland Airport.

She will never fly again.

On the morning of the crash, Joan had opened her eyes, greeted by the bright sunlight which came through her east bedroom window. Fully awake, still she lay there, her body tired from the busy day before. She had rushed around trying to exchange some Christmas gifts for David, but the after-holiday selection had been discouraging and she didn't feel her efforts had been successful.

She hadn't set the alarm. She lay there for a moment, hoping that the warm sunlight sifting through the curtains would somehow give her enough energy to arise, shake off the lethargy of post-Christmas inertia and get things done that she needed to do before leaving for the airport.

She had a couple of errands to accomplish on her way, but she needed to check in at Stapleton Field around 2 P.M. She was anxious to get back to David. This was the first time she had flown during the holidays for quite a few years. After fifteen years as a stewardess she had acquired enough seniority to book flights which gave her plenty of time off around the holidays. This year was different. She sighed. If only Mark had met his financial obligations, she wouldn't be in such a financial bind. She hated to leave David, even with Uncle Stan and Aunt Louise. But she had no choice. She needed the money. Mark hadn't paid child support—in fact he hadn't even attempted to see the boy in twenty-two months. She had initiated legal action against him for back support.

She turned on her side, trying to enjoy her last minutes in bed. It was no use. She was worried about the suit. Mark always retaliated whenever anyone crossed him. She was afraid that he would try to get even with her through David. In the past he often used David as a pawn.

It was time to get up. She wasn't resting anyway. She stretched her aching joints, turned on some music and took a shower. She spent most of the morning packing items for the move to California, remembering to switch on her telephone recorder. There were just a couple of messages, mostly from friends wishing her a happy holiday. She quickly reset the recorder, dressed and left the house, with enough time to make her scheduled stops on the way to the airport.

The sun was bright, but it was a typical, clear, cold day. The snow crunched under her feet as she walked out to check her mailbox, and she pulled out of the driveway about 11:00 A.M. Her old Firebird was still giving her trouble. It finally started but it sputtered and choked like an asthmatic crow even though she had left it running for some time last night.

The shopping center was still mobbed with people. It was a hassle but she made a couple of exchanges, one at the department store and another at the drug store, picking up a sale item for David, a velour Santa formed like a snowman in chubby sections. He would love it!

She rushed to her car and turned toward the belt route, Highway 25. The car was still vibrating. As she picked up speed, she decided she would have to take it back to the garage on January 6th when she returned. There was something wrong with the frame, she thought, as it shimmied along at 50 miles per hour. Darn. Why didn't they fix it right the first time? This was a nuisance.

She pulled into the enclosed parking lot, revved up the engine, turned off the key, then grabbed her flight bag and suitcase. On second thought, she opened the trunk to check her spare tire and to make sure she put her jumper cables back. Jumpers were standard equipment for flight crews when they lived in a climate like Denver. Sometimes after only one night, a car had to be jumped. When you were away several days, it was a certainty.

She hurried into the terminal and checked in. Operations informed her that Flight 173 was on schedule. Hurriedly she made preparations. The entire crew would change in Denver, the Denver-based crew would fly to Portland, turn around and come right back to Denver. Joan would catch the 8:05 flight to Salt Lake City to spend the rest of the holidays. Anticipating her return, she began to feel less resentful about selling her vacation.

The airport was still reeling from the crush of holiday travelers. Families traveled together this time of year, as opposed to the dominance of businessmen the rest of the year. Seeing the travelers, Joan was even more anxious to get back to Utah. She had picked up some popcorn ball molds for David. She smiled when she recalled her promise to the boy. They would go right out and buy some Jolly Time Pop Corn—Uncle Stan was the marketer for Jolly Time in Utah, and David wouldn't hear of their buying any other kind. David was looking forward to making the balls—he never forgot anything like that. And, to be truthful, she was, too. Besides, she could tease Uncle Stan about his product. That was good fun. She almost made him mad once, calling him the Tabasco Kid.

He marketed Tabasco, too, and used the product liberally, even on—ugh—scrambled eggs! She grinned when she thought about it. She had tried it, and it tasted good!

With a light heart she started her shift. The flight started out no differently from other flights, except for the typical holiday passengers. Their festive mood made Joan even more excited about the toys she had exchanged for David. She couldn't restrain from showing some of them to other crew members. The anticipation of David's reaction lessened the agony of their separation.

Flight 173 was enroute to Portland with 181 passengers and eight crew members aboard. Cruising at 35,000 feet, the flight was routine. Joan was walking aft in the first class passenger cabin when she felt the forward thrust of the aircraft suddenly diminish. That signalled her that they were beginning to descend, in preparation for a landing. She hurried to complete her duties.

In the cockpit, at 1705:47, the captain called Portland Approach and advised them that their altitude was 10,000 feet. They had to reduce their air speed. Portland responded, telling them to maintain their heading for a visual approach to runway 28. Flight 173 answered, "We have the field in sight."

At 1707:55, Portland Approach instructed the flight to descend and maintain 8,000 feet. The flight responded, acknowledging instructions. At 1709:40, Flight 173 acknowledged clearance to continue its descent to 6,000 feet. As they began this last descent, they lowered the landing gear. There was a loud noise and a severe jolt. Joan felt it in the cabin. So did the passengers. Suddenly their merriment ceased. An eerie silence fell over the entire cabin. Almost everyone aboard was aware that this was unusual. But the stewardesses quickly regained their composure and went about their duties as if nothing had happened. Joan was the coolest of all. After all, she set the pace as senior flight attendant.

Portland Approach had meanwhile advised the captain to contact them for landing, but he replied in the negative, informing them that he had a gear problem. This was the first indication to anyone on the ground that Flight 173 was in trouble. They responded at 1712:28: "United one seven three heavy roger, maintain 5,000. Turn left, heading two zero zero." At 1714:43 they continued instructions: "Turn left heading one zero zero and I'll just orbit you out of there until you get your problem under control."

About this time Joan entered the cockpit. Captain McBroom discussed the problem with her and told her that after they ran a few more checks, he would let her know what he intended to do. Joan proceeded back to the cabin, reassuring passengers who appeared upset, but then she decided the captain should know about the passengers' uneasiness. As a consequence, he went on the intercom and made his announcement. He concluded, "Let me repeat, this is just precautionary and there is no cause for alarm."

At 1738 Flight 173 contacted the United Airlines Systems Maintenance Control Center in San Francisco, California. Through air-to-ground radio the captain explained his situation to the company dispatch and told them what he had done about it, insisting that the gear was fully extended. He stated his intention to hold for another fifteen or twenty minutes, but he was going to instruct the flight attendants to prepare the passengers for any emergency evacuation that might become necessary.

At 1744:03 United San Francisco radioed: "Okay, United one seven three. You estimate that you'll make a landing about five minutes past the hour. Is that okay?"

The captain responded, "Ya, that's good ballpark. I am not gonna hurry the girls. We got about a hundred-and-sixty-five people on board and we...want to...take our time and get everybody ready and then we will go. It's clear as a bell and no problem."

From 1744:30 until about 1745:23 the cockpit voice recorder taped the conversation between the captain and the first flight attendant concerning passenger preparation in crash landing and evacuation procedures. At 1744:41 Joan said to the captain: "That's the only thing I need from you right now."

The captain responded, "Okay. What would you do? Have you got any suggestions about when to brace and what to do on the P.A.?"

Joan countered with, "I...I'll be honest with you. I have never had one of these before. This is my first."

At 1748:58 the fuel pump lights in the cockpit started to blink. At 1751:35 the captain advised the flight engineer to contact United Airlines representative and tell him about the situation, that they would land with about 4,000 pounds of fuel. At 1753:30 the captain told ground, "I'll land about five after." Taped recordings of the last minutes of conversation between crew members tell the traumatic story:

At 1806:19, the first flight attendant entered the cockpit. The captain asked, "How you doing?" She responded, "Well, I think we're ready." At this time the aircraft was about 17 miles south of the airport on a southwesterly heading. The conversation between the first flight attendant and the captain continued until about 1806:40 when the captain said, "Okay. We're going to go in now. We should be landing in about five minutes." Almost simultaneous with this comment, the first officer said, "I think you just lost number four...." followed immediately by advice to the flight engineer, "...better get some crossfeeds open there or something."

At 1806:46, the first officer told the captain, "We're going to lose an engine...." The captain replied, "Why?" At 1806:49, the first officer again stated, "We're losing an engine." Again the captain asked, "Why?" The first officer responded, "Fuel."

Between 1806:52 and 1807:06, the CVR revealed conflicting and confusing conversation between flight crewmembers as to the aircraft's fuel state. At 1807:06, the first officer said, "It's flamed out."

At 1807:12, the captain called Portland Approach and requested, "...would like clearance for an approach into two eight left, now." The aircraft was about 19 mi south southwest of the airport and turning left. This was the first request for an approach clearance from Flight 173 since the landing gear problem began. Portland Approach immediately gave the flight vectors for a visual approach to runway 28L. The flight turned toward the vector heading of 010.

From 1807:27 until 1809:16, the following intracockpit conversation took place:

1807:27—Flight Engineer: "We're going to lose number three in a minute, too."

1807:31—Flight Engineer: "It's showing zero."

Captain: "You got a thousand pounds. You got to."

Flight Engineer: "Five thousand in there...but we lost it."

Captain: "Alright."

1807:38—Flight Engineer: "Are you getting it back?"

18:07:40—First Officer: "No number four. You got that crossfeed open?"

1807:41—Flight Engineer: "No, I haven't got it open. Which one?"

1807:42—Captain: "Open 'em both—get some fuel in there. Got some fuel pressure?"

Flight Engineer: "Yes, sir."

1807:48—Captain: "Rotation. Now she's coming."

1807:52—Captain: "Okay, watch one and two. We're showing down to zero or a thousand."

Flight Engineer: "Yeah."

Captain: "On number one?"

Flight Engineer: "Right."

1808:08—First Officer: "Still not getting it."

1808:11—Captain: "Well, open all four crossfeeds."

Flight Engineer: "All four?"

Captain: "Yeah."

1808:14—First Officer: "Alright, now it's coming."

1808:19—First Officer: "It's going to be—on approach though."

Unknown voice: "Yeah."

1808:42—Captain: "You gotta keep 'em running..."

Flight Engineer: "Yes, sir."

1808:45—First Officer: "Get this...on the ground."

Flight Engineer: "Yeah. It's showing not very much more fuel."

1809:16—Flight Engineer: "We're down to one on the totalizer. Number two is empty."

At 1809:21, the captain advised Portland Approach, "United, one seven three is going to turn toward the airport and come in." After confirming Flight 173's intentions, Portland Approach cleared the flight for visual approach to runway 28L.

At 1810:17, the captain requested that the flight engineer "reset that circuit breaker momentarily. See if we get gear lights." The flight engineer complied with the request.

At 1810:47, the captain requested the flight's distance from the airport. Portland Approach responded, "Twelve flying miles." The flight was then cleared to contact Portland tower.

At 1813:21, the flight engineer stated, "We've lost two engines, guys." At 1813:25, he stated, "We just lost two engines—one and two."

At 1813:38, the captain said, "They're all going. We can't

make Troutdale." The first officer said, "We can't make anything."

It was seven minutes after Joan left the cockpit before the first officer gave out a Mayday to the Portland tower. "Portland tower, United 173 heavy, Mayday. We're—the engines are flaming out. We're going down. We're not going to be able to make the airport." This was the last transmission from Flight 173.

After the fuel lights started blinking, the plane was approximately seventeen miles away from the airport. Still, it would continue to circle out to twenty miles away, then back to seventeen and out to twenty, for seven more crucial minutes.

Investigations of the crash revealed that the pilot thought he had enough fuel to land the crippled airliner. His computations apparently were faulty—and a number of his crew tried to communicate this information to him in the final moments preceeding the crash. From findings of the National Transportation Safety Board, Washington, D.C.:

> Admittedly, the abnormal rear extension was cause for concern and a flightcrew should assess the situation before communicating with the dispatch at maintenance personnel. However, aside from the crew's discussing the problem and adhering to the DC-8 Flight Manual, the only remaining step was to contact company dispatch and line maintenance. From the time the captain informed Portland Approach of the gear problem until contact with company dispatch and line maintenance, about 28 minutes had elapsed. The irregular gear check procedures contained in their manual were brief, the weather was good, the area was void of heavy traffic, and there were no additional problems experienced by the flight that would have delayed the captain's communicating with the company. The company maintenance staff verified

that everything possible had been done to assure the integrity of the landing gear. Therefore, upon termination of communications with company dispatch and maintenance personnel, which was about 30 min before the crash, the captain could have made a landing attempt. The Safety Board believes that Flight 173 could have landed safely within 30 to 40 min after the landing gear malfunction.

Upon completing communications with company line and dispatch, the captain called the first flight attendant to the cockpit to instruct her to prepare the cabin for a possible abnormal landing. During the ensuing discussion, the captain did not assign the first flight attendant a specified time within which to prepare the cabin, as required by the flight manual. In the absence of such time constraint, the first flight attendant was probably left with the impression that time efficiency was not necessarily as important as the assurance of thorough preparation.

The Safety Board believes that any time a flight deviates from a flight plan, the flightcrew should evaluate the potential effect of such deviation on the aircraft fuel status. This flightcrew knew that the evaluation of the landing gear problem and preparation for an emergency landing would require extended holding before landing.

The flightcrew should have been aware that there were 46,700 lbs of fuel aboard the aircraft when it left Denver at 1433 and that there was about 45,650 lbs at takeoff at 1447. Regardless of whether they were aware of the actual fuel quantities, they certainly should have been aware that the initial fuel load was predicated on fuel consumption for the planned 2 hr 26 min en route flight, plus a reserve which includes sufficient fuel for 45 min at normal cruise and a contingency margin of about 20 min additional flight.

Therefore, the crew should have been concerned that fuel could become critical after holding. Proper crew management includes constant awareness of fuel remaining as it relates to time. In fact, the Safety Board believes that proper planning would provide for enough fuel on landing for a go-around should it become necessary. Such planning should also consider possible fuel-quantity indication inaccuracies. This would necessitate establishing a deadline time for initiating the approach and constant monitoring of time, as well as the aircraft's position relative to the active runway. Such procedures should be routine for all flightcrews. However, based on available evidence, this flightcrew did not adhere to such procedures. On the contrary, the cockpit conversation indicates insufficient attention and a lack of awareness on the part of the captain about the aircraft's fuel state after entering and even after a prolonged period of holding. The other two flight crewmembers, although they made several comments regarding the aircraft's fuel state, did not express direct concern regarding the amount of time remaining to total fuel exhaustion. While there is evidence to indicate that the crew was aware of the amount of fuel remaining at various times, there is no evidence that the onboard quantity was monitored in relation to time remaining during the final 30 min of flight. The Safety Board believes that had the flightcrew been aware of the fuel state, comments concerning time to fuel exhaustion would have been voiced. However, there was none until after the aircraft was already in a position from which recovery was not possible.

In analyzing the flightcrew's actions, the Safety Board considered that the crew could have been misled by inaccuracies within the fuel-quantity measuring system. However, those intracockpit comments and radio transmissions in which fuel quantity was mentioned indicate that the fuel-quantity indicating system was accurate.

Had the flightcrew related any of these fuel quantities to fuel flow, they should have been aware that fuel exhaustion would occur at or about 1815. Other evidence that the captain had failed to assess the effect of continued holding on fuel on board. Just minutes earlier, at 1748:56, he was made aware that only 5,000 lbs remained. During the 16 min between the observation of 5,000 lbs and 1805, the aircraft would consume at least 3,000 lbs of fuel. Further evidence of the flightcrew's lack of concern of awareness was provided just after his observations of 4,000 lbs remaining about 17 min before the crash, when the first officer left the cockpit at the captain's request to check on the cabin emergency evacuation preparations. Upon his return, about 4 min later, he gave the captain an estimate of another 2 or 3 min for the completion of the cabin preparation. At this time, the aircraft was in the general vicinity of the airport. In the initial interview with the captain, he stated that he felt the cabin preparation could be completed in from 10 to 15 min and that the "tail end of it" could be accomplished on the final approach to the airport. Certainly there was nothing more to do in the cockpit. All of the landing gear check procedures, as prescribed in the approved flight manual and recommended by company line maintenance, had been completed and dispatch had been notified and had alerted Portland company personnel of the problems.

Under these circumstances, there appears to have been no valid reason not to continue their heading inbound toward the airport in order to make their previously estimated landing time. However, about 1801:12, the first officer accepted and the captain did not question a vector heading which would take them away from the airport and delay their landing time appreciably. Moreover, after the turn was completed none of the flightcrew suggested turning toward the airport. Thus, it was at this time that the crew's continuing preoccupation with the landing gear problem and landing preparations became crucial and an accident became inevitable.

The plane fell just six miles away from landing, when the engines flamed out from lack of fuel. The pilot chose the best place available for a crash landing. Instead of a busy freeway or a residential area, the plane slammed to earth in a grove of trees where two unoccupied houses stood waiting under darkening skies.

In trying to determine the cause of the crash, the National Transportation Safety Board listed "human factor" as the culprit, stating that the crew had no idea until the last terrifying minutes before the crash that the plane was running out of fuel.

"Boy, that fuel sure went to hell all of a sudden," had exclaimed Flight Officer Forrest E. Mendenhall on a tape reviewed by the board. Officer Mendenhall was one of the ten who did not survive.

Over a year ago, after that fateful crash, Nancy King related the following:

For two weeks after the accident I felt Joan's presence with me all of the time, during the day, no matter what I was doing, and even at night. I don't know exactly why she picked me except that we were quite close. Although we had flown together only a month, we had a lot in common. We had both gone through a divorce, I had a child about the same age as David, and furthermore, I had experienced about the same kinds of problems with my ex-husband as she had with Mark. Joan and I were both concerned about our children, in the event that something happened to us. The main difference between us was the fact that I was newly married and very happy. She seemed drawn to me because of this, too.

Over the period of two weeks I felt uneasy because of her constant presence. Finally I discussed it with my husband. He was aware of my discomfort, but he knew I had just undergone a traumatic situation with the accident and would have to acclimate myself to flying again. When I disclosed what was really bothering me, he did not hesitate for a minute.

"Why do you think Joan is staying so close to you, Nancy?"

I was hard pressed for an answer, but I analyzed the problem as well as I could. "Everything happened so fast. No one had a chance to prepare for it—or even to think about it. Maybe she is upset because she doesn't know actually what happened. Maybe...maybe she needs some answers." It was the best I could do.

His reply was direct and to the point. "Then explain it to her."

It seemed like a logical move. We went into the livingroom, sat on the couch, and I began to talk to Joan. "It was a mistake, Joan. A dumb mistake. We ran out of gas. I don't understand how a thing like that could have happened, but it did. You and the first officer were killed, Joan, along with several others, and we are really sorry about that, but there is nothing we can do about it. There is nothing YOU can do about it now. You did everything you could. Please don't worry. Everything is O.K. David is being cared for."

I told her all of the details about the crash. I tried to reassure her. Almost immediately after I finished, Joan's presence left me, and I have never felt it since that time. She seemed satisfied with my explanation. I hope she is content. She deserves some happiness, somewhere.

The Disrespect of Last Respects

Joan's viewing and services were unforgettable. I will never forget the onset of 1979. New Years is supposed to be a time of new beginnings and if any family needed a new beginning it was ours. Such was not to be. Even at the funeral we couldn't put aside our animosities. I tried, for Joan's sake, but there were too many complications, too much greed and avarice, too much vindictiveness for a peaceful farewell. And I didn't have much help.

I had to break the news to David. How do you tell a boy under four that his mother is never coming home? We told him that her flight had been delayed. He could accept that, temporarily, but twice he asked, "Is this the day my Mama's coming in?"

I put him off both times with, "No, she won't be coming in today."

But eventually he had to be told. Here was a child who had lost the two people closest to him in a little over a year. He still remembered his grandmother, "Ma" as he called her.

Whenever he saw a yellow volkswagon, he would holler, "There goes Ma's car!" She had died almost fourteen months earlier. No, I couldn't tell him his mother was gone, too. Not yet.

On the evening of the viewing at the mortuary, we arrived a little early. We wanted to check Joan's clothing to see that she was properly dressed. Before the others arrived, we closed and sealed the casket as Joan had requested.

Dave and Shauna came in about half an hour after the viewing began and stayed completely away from the rest of the family. I wasn't surprised. For people who had stolen her inheritance (I had proof of this) and taunted and degraded her all of her life, they had a lot of nerve even showing up at Joan's viewing. My daughter Micalle later voiced these same sentiments at Joan's funeral.

What I didn't know was that they were already making plans to break Joan's will. No wonder they laughed and talked as if nothing had happened. It was a field day for them. Their loss was slight and they thought there was a chance for gain. Why wouldn't they laugh?

I was heart-broken. When Dave's mother and father came through the line, I looked Henrietta Young straight in the eyes and said, "Mrs. Young, I've heard from United Airlines, and a coroner in Portland. If there is anything you want to know about Joan's remains or the circumstances of her death, feel free to ask me. I would be glad to tell you anything you want to know."

I fully expected her to be shocked. I didn't think she knew anything about the phone calls. Instead she turned beet red, stammered a lot, and then said, "Shauna was right there beside me. I only made those calls at her request."

Surprised at her admission, I was embarrassed about the humiliation she was suffering at my statements. The questions had not originated with Shauna; they were a product of a legal mind. Who else but Mrs. Young's son Dave?

There were some ugly insinuations made about Dave and Shauna at the mortuary that night. —Not by me, although I certainly felt like it. They were made openly and loudly by some people not members of the family—and later attributed to me! Shauna and Dave no doubt heard them—everyone did—and decided to add these obscenities to their case against me. In view of all they had done to Joan, this time they could have shown a little class. They failed completely. I will never understand how anyone could carry such greed and feelings of revenge to a funeral.

I wasn't in good shape, I'll admit. I hadn't slept for days, and that night was no different. How could I break the news to David? How could I tell him so that he could accept it and yet not be broken by the loss? It was a heavy load, one that I did not feel wise enough to handle. Furthermore, the next day was Joan's services—and Louise's birthday. It would be a lot easier to dispel memories of such times if they did not occur on days which you try to remember.

On Monday I had received a call from one of the television stations asking how I felt about their filming part of Joan's services to put on their newscast. I told them we would rather keep the funeral private. Anything connected with Joan was newsworthy, even her funeral.

It was difficult to keep things as Joan wanted them. Earlier the television and radio stations had called and asked about Joan and David. Two of the television stations asked when I expected Joan's remains to arrive in Salt Lake City, and if it was all right for them to televise what they referred to as "her last flight." I requested that they not do so. And right after one of the news shows related details of the crash that took Joan's life, a reporter from the *Salt Lake Tribune* called. "Are you Joan Wheeler's uncle?" she asked.

"Yes, I am," I replied.

"Well, what's up with her sister, Shauna Young?" She had called Shauna to learn more details about Joan's death and

Shauna had retorted, "Well, why don't you ask her uncle, Stan Mann."

Sensing a story, the girl asked why the boy had been given to me, and not to the sister. I explained briefly that there were family estrangements that had never been resolved.

All of the complications of the past few days had been caused by greed. I was certain that Mark's sudden paternal interest was because of the insurance money and David's trust, and I later found out that Shauna's interest was focused on her attempt to subvert and destroy even her sister's dying wishes—and in her husband's representation of Mark in a wrongful death suit and an attempt to break the trust.

Both of them felt they had a good chance to profit from Joan's death. When Joan and Mark divorced, Joan had a $140,000 insurance policy with United and a $64,000 policy with New York Life, the latter double indemnity. However, because Mark had not paid any support money and Joan had been in a financial bind with her new home, she had reduced her New York Life policy to $25,000, and double indemnity was not in effect for a member of the crew.

Her total estate was approximately $225,000, not the half million that Mark continually claimed. I had told him this and Joan's attorney talked to his attorney, but they weren't convinced, perhaps because Mark's attorney was his new wife's brother-in-law, Wayne Wadsworth. Mark also figured he could sue United or the airplane manufacturer for a big sum, but later the accident was declared a result of human error and the maximum any member of the crew could sue for was $25,000. Mark's mind worked by greed, not by reason, and I was soon to learn this first hand. When United refused to give Mark official notice of Joan's death, he had his attorney call to demand such notification. They both failed.

By this time I was beginning to believe everything Joan had told me, no matter how far out it seemed. Since Mark had threatened to come to Salt Lake to get the boy, I called the sheriff's office and made arrangements for Deputy Kunz to be at my home during the time of Joan's service. My bishop's wife was coming over to care for David, but I wanted the deputy there, too, in case Mark tried to pull some of the tricks he was noted for.

Officer Kunz arrived at 8:15, about an hour before we were to leave. He was a personable man and won David over right away. David was having a great time looking at the deputy's gun as we left.

Shortly after we arrived at the mortuary, Marilyn McArthur and Joan's supervisor from United Airlines walked in. They had flown in from Denver to attend the services. I went into the corridor, and noticed my youngest son talking to Dave Young. I called him over and asked him to come with me. Dave started to talk to me but I told him I did not care to speak with him. He wouldn't take no for an answer, so after a brief conversation I finally turned to him and said, "Dave, let's face it. You are a liar and you are married to a liar. I don't care to waste my time when I know that you are standing there lying to me. You insult my intelligence by thinking I don't know it!" Then I walked away.

Later on, in letters from Wayne Wadsworth, I was accused of making statements other than these, and of using vulgar language.

At the service Dave cornered Marilyn McArthur. Marilyn came to the viewing on behalf of the airlines, and Dave tried to pump her for information without success. I didn't know the gist of their conversation, but I was certain he was "gathering evidence." Dave wasn't one to let an opportunity pass him by. Marilyn later said that United had never had this kind of situation over a fatality before. She wondered what was going on. I thought I knew, but it had only begun.

My daughter, Micalle, who had been very close to Joan, told Shauna, "I can't see how you even had the nerve to come here after the way you were with Joan."

Shauna retaliated with a frosty, "I have every damn right to be here."

Then as I entered the room and took my daughter by the arm, Shauna said "I don't want to hear anymore from you damn assholes." I am ashamed for these incidents and I wish they had not happened, especially during a sacred occasion like a funeral. But I did not have much help in trying to make it a dignified ceremony and my philosophy has never been peace at the sacrifice of principles.

During the service Byron Fisher filed for us to have temporary custody of David and Judge Christine Durham granted this motion, but that evening I received a call from Bishop T. Ken Peterson in Denver, who had heard from a friend of Joan's in Michigan who claimed that Joan wanted her to take David in case of Joan's death. She also said that there was another will which Joan had only recently made out and they would find it in her house. I knew nothing about it but I instructed Bishop Peterson to get the lawyer who had done some work for Joan and, if they would, to go over the house thoroughly to see if they could locate a will.

Another matter involved Mark's new bishop in California. Mark had sought his bishop's help in getting his son from the "terrible uncle" who was keeping him away from the boy. Mark had told Bishop William Treu that he consulted with Bishop Peterson about his son previously. This was not true. Mark had never talked to Bishop Peterson, although if he'd been interested, he could have. He had his address and telephone number. Bishop Peterson asked the other church leader if he knew what was required for Mark to get back his standing in the church: he was to meet his financial obligations to the boy, and this he had never done. He also asked how well he knew Mark and his new wife. Bishop Treu admitted this was the first time he had met Mark even though Mark and Sylvi had lived in his ward for fourteen months.

Some months later this bishop gave a deposition under

oath in Encino, California, that indicated entirely contradictory testimony. He either lied to Bishop Peterson or he perjured himself in court, and lying carries the same weight whether you are a leader or a follower.—Or maybe it doesn't. I think a bishop might be held even more accountable.

After Bishop Peterson's call, Louise and I remembered that we had close friends in the same area of California who had known Mark and Joan well, so we decided to call them and explain what had happened. It turned out they knew Bishop Treu personally and wouldn't mind calling and talking to him about "that terrible uncle in Utah."

I dreaded the next day. I knew I had to face the situation with David. It couldn't be delayed any longer. I also had a number of things that had to be settled at the office and I had to fly to Denver to check on Joan's house. Marilyn McArthur told me some things which had happened to the homes of victims of airline crashes. It was common that their keys or driver's license or other I.D. disappeared, and then, later, scavengers picked them up, went to the houses and looted them.—And lights had been seen on in Joan's house. I determined to go to Denver the next morning.

At my invitation Bishop Kerry Heinz and his wife Beverly came to our home that afternoon. I needed fortification for the task at hand. We talked for a while, then I asked David to come and sit on my lap. I had worried and prayed about this matter for a number of days, and now that the time for telling him was at hand, I offered one last silent prayer.

I put my arms around David and played our little love game, then I said, "David, there has been a bad accident, and Heavenly Father, knowing that your mother couldn't get well, has decided that since she was such a wonderful mother, He needed her help in heaven. She has gone to join Ma."

David just looked at us. We couldn't tell what he was feeling. I went on. "Your mama had asked Grandma and me if you could come and live with us. We would take care of you and have you for our little boy, and we were delighted with this plan. So from now on, David, you will be our little boy and live here with us. Micalle will be your sister and you will have Brett, Randon and Scott for your very own brothers."

Finally David looked at me. "Isn't Mama ever coming back?"

Through the lump in my throat I answered, "We will see Mama some day when we go back to our Heavenly Father, but she won't be coming back here. That is why you are going to live with us. Grandma and I will be your mama and daddy."

His little body shuddered, a feeling I will never forget. He looked at me with trusting eyes and said, "I want you for my daddy, but I want my mama to come home."

I tried to explain that she had work to do with Heavenly Father, then we got down on the floor and played a while. His attention turned to Beverly Heinz, and I returned to the couch. Soon he came over to me and inquired, "Am I going to live with you forever and ever?" I told him yes, and that when we all went back to Heavenly Father, we would all live together, his mama, "Ma," and all the rest of us. He seemed satisfied and went back to play.

When Micalle came in from school, he ran up to her and said, "Micalle, you are going to be my sister and I am going to be your brother forever and ever." He was excited about it. He repeated the same idea when Brett came home.

I could not foresee any possibility of anyone's pulling this boy away from the heart of our home. He was happy here. He knew us and loved us. Next to his mother we were the only family he had. His father had deserted him three years before and completely abdicated his responsibilities to the boy. He had shown no interest in David. Surely he would never want him. It was inconceivable. He would not tear the boy out of the only environment he knew, no matter what the enticement. I was wrong.

The next morning I caught a plane to Denver. Bishop Peterson met me at the airport. Although we had never met before I felt I knew him well because of our conversations on the telephone and because of what Joan had told me. A large man, about 6'3", with an athletic build and a warm, friendly smile, he drove me out to Joan's house, telling me on the way that he and the attorney had not been able to find another will, even though they had searched the house thoroughly.

Arriving at the house was a bit of a trauma for me. I walked into a house that had not been lived in since early December when Joan left to visit Virginia and her husband. Furthermore, she was in the middle of a big move, but nothing was in disarray. The house looked as if someone had just cleaned and left momentarily. Hanging on the refrigerator door at eye level were four inspirational thoughts. One was on the sacred responsibility of parenthood, another on teaching righteousness by example, and still another defined integrity. The last one treated the subject of influencing your son to want to go out and preach the gospel.

Bishop Peterson and I spent most of the day going through Joan's things, looking for another will or any paper that might indicate Joan's wishes. We found nothing; however there were stacks of boxes in the garage and in the basement, in anticipation of her move. (United permitted her to take as much as 500 pounds of goods on each trip to California and she was taking advantage of this in order to reduce her moving bill.) Naturally we did not have time to go through all of this.

Before I left I noted other signs of conscientious motherhood. Posted on the fridge was a little chart with squares marked off for each day of the week. In each square was a notation of something David had done to help around the house. Up in David's bedroom was another chart showing the days that David had picked up his toys, made his own bed, hung up his clothes and other helpful chores. In the drawer next to Joan's bed I found files filled with articles relating to various gospel principles. And on the nightstand itself was her Bible, with a letter my wife had written her as a bookmark. I read the letter. Louise told Joan how much we loved her and how greatly we were looking forward to their visit for the holidays. My eyes brimmed over as I made my way down to the family room. Here in the magazine rack I discovered all kinds of pamphlets and advice on how to handle an adopted child and on raising a child as a single parent.

I spent the whole time learning to fully appreciate the niece I thought I knew. There was a dimension of her life I had never explored, a dimension I had not been aware of. No wonder she didn't take my advice when I told her to consider an apartment or a condominium instead of a house, in order to cut down expenses. It was important for her to live in a nice home in a good neighborhood because of David. Only then, after looking through her house and realizing the extent of her devotion to the boy's future, did I realize that money was only a means to insure David's happiness and proper development. That was what she worked for: to provide for her son.

What a different world this would be if all children could experience the kind of love and devotion that Joan exhibited for her son. I later read a blessing given to Joan over twenty years earlier when she was told that a wonderful privilege and opportunity would come her way which would bring great joy and happiness into her life, and this would be brought about by her love for a little child. Now I fully understood how she had worked for this relationship, how she had nurtured it, developed it, day by day, act by act, word by word, with total dedication to this boy. Few children with two parents enjoy the benefits which David received.

The whole tragedy was so senseless. Joan did not want to move to Denver. She was forced into the move by a selfish, greedy man who would not leave her alone, even after he was married to another woman. He played with her life, tried to hurt her through David, and he never cared enough about David to send support money. She had sold her Christmas vacation in order to meet bills and found herself in another stewardess' place on a flight with a captain who repeatedly ignored warnings regarding his fuel situation. If it hadn't been so tragic, it would have seemed preposterous.

I still ask myself, why Joan? I had known that my sister's marriage was not a happy one and that Joan attached herself to my family in order to avoid unhappiness at home. We had always been very close, but imagine my surprise when I opened Joan's files and found a more complete scrapbook of my life than I myself had kept. I began to see how her life related to ours. She was indeed our daughter. She attached herself to us by more than blood. She cared, she truly cared, about us and our activities and our desires.

I knew now why I had to act in Joan's behalf. It was not simply that she had asked me to do so, though that would have been reason enough. It entailed family ties as strong as any I had ever felt. I began to see the effect of Joan's life on our family, and I hoped that we had given her some good moments. She certainly had suffered in her few years on earth. Perhaps we had managed, through our bungling but obviously sincere efforts, to show her we cared, to transmit the love we felt.

As I sat on the couch in her family room, I earnestly prayed that we had added to her life's treasury of good memories. I picked up a copy of her personal history and read snatches of it. The account was written in her own handwriting. But she had never finished it. It stopped in 1973, the time when Mark abandoned her the first time.

The brilliant sunlight shone through the window in Joan's house and I became more and more aware that Joan was never coming home again.

Or perhaps she was already home. I hoped so.

First the Mother, Then the Son

In the midst of all this confusion and legal hassle, little David was torn from our home by Mark whose "natural rights" prevailed—even though he had fraudulently adopted the boy, left the adoptive mother (who subsequently was granted custody), and abandoned them both on the very day the adoption became legal.

David didn't know Mark when he came to pick him up. He screamed and fought all the way out to the car. We were the only family he knew—he would have preferred to go home with his mother but since he couldn't, he wanted to stay with his "Grandpa." He was making a good adjustment to Joan's death. He had our children, his aunts and cousins with whom he was well acquainted, and he was living in surroundings familiar to him.

In July of 1979, we went to court to try to regain custody of David. We learned he had regressed to an infantile state. He was crawling on his hands and knees, he spoke only in disrupted speech patterns, and had become an inveterate liar. His pediatrician prescribed tranquilizers to be administered four times a day. I couldn't believe this was the same child we held in our arms only six months earlier. That sturdy, robust little man!

Our attorney was unable to assert any evidence of relationship between the boy and ourselves; consequently David was awarded to the custody of Mark and his new wife Sylvi, whom the doctor commended for having done a remarkable job with David. In view of the fact that Mark had been critically shot after David went to live with the Wheelers, I would assume that any degree of "stabilizing" was remarkable. What a situation for a boy only four years old!

The hearing brought out a number of facts that appalled me. First, it seemed that Sylvi and Wadsworth (her brother-in-law, remember) had "bought" the testimony of an incompetent doctor whose words simply aped Sylvi's and Mark's opinions. Second, the Wheelers had obviously prompted the boy to respond in a negative way toward Joan, Louise, and me. Third, the Wheelers seemed to be the doctor's only source of information. Not only had he made no effort to get to the bottom of David's problem, he was actually misinformed. The doctor testified under oath that David saw his father shot, but Mark testified under oath at a later date that this was not so. In short, the doctor simply reinforced Mark's attitude toward Joan, and, as a matter of record, the doctor's testimony was largely made up of quotations from Sylvi.

The last time I saw Mark at the time of the divorce settlement, when he tried to pick up the house check, he appeared extreme in dress. Louise didn't even recognize him. His hair was long and he had a string of beads around his neck. On January 11th he cleaned up. This was the custody hearing and apparently he went to a lot of trouble to look conservative. Obviously other preparations had been made for the hearing as well.

The Wheelers' main witness was Doctor Robert H. Marshall, whose testimony cut me to the quick. I couldn't believe how one-sided this hearing was. I learned things that hurt me terribly about David, but what hurt most was the Wheelers' and Wadsworth's attempts to misdirect the court. And, unfortunately for David, they succeeded. Portions of the transcripts are worth repeating.

Mr. Wadsworth questioned Dr. Marshall, the Wheelers' pediatrician. After establishing what sounded like an impressive background for the doctor, the examination continued.

Q   Since your practice here in Encino have you become acquainted with the Wheeler family, Mark and Sylvi Wheeler?

A   Yes. Approximately 20 months ago Mrs. Wheeler came into the office. She was pregnant at the time. She was introduced to me as a future patient by one of my patients, and I met her at that time for the first time.

Q   Was that for the purpose of determining if you would be the physician to take care of her child when it was born?

A   Yes.

Q   Did that situation mature and did you in fact become the attending physician for her first child when it was born?

A   Yes.

Q   What is his name?

A   His name, right now it is a total block. Christopher.* I'm sorry.

Q   And so you first became acquainted with their family as being the physician for Christopher?

A   Right.

Q   And you have continued in that capacity up to the present time?

A   Yes, I have.

(*The child's name was Mark Christopher.)

Q Then subsequently were you contacted with respect to Mr. Wheeler's adopted son, David, when he came to live with the Wheeler family?

A Yes. Apparently the day after David arrived in California Mrs. Wheeler called me and asked me if I would examine the child to make certain that he was in good physical condition, and I did so, I believe it was January 13—January 9, 1979.

Q As a result of that examination what did you find with respect to David?

A In physical condition the boy was in excellent physical condition, but he was extremely tense and he was suffering at that moment from a separation anxiety, his mother apparently having died very shortly before that period of time.

Q After you first saw David did you and Mrs. Wheeler make attempts to determine his past medical history from prior treating physicians?

A Yes, I had a consultation with both Mr. and Mrs. Wheeler in January some four days after I saw the boy. We reviewed the situation, and I was informed at that time that the mother of the boy had told him that his father was dead and that much of the anxiety apparently arising from this circumstance was from the fact that he presumed that Mark Wheeler was dead.

Dr. Marshall then referred to limited attempts to locate other doctors who had treated David. Then he went on to relate his own contacts with him.

Q In your professional judgment do you deem it important to determine what this prior medical history may be?

A Well, considering the extreme anxiety that the boy showed and considering in light of what he has told me since then, I think it is very important, because the boy is obviously suffering from great anxiety and it would be helpful to know just what his state was prior to this.

Q   Then when was the next time that you saw David?

A   Well, I saw David on several occasions while Christopher was coming into the office, and he seemed to be calming down very nicely. He was friendly, playful, had no difficulties whatsoever, but I did not actually examine him. This was just contact in the office when he came with his new brother.

I saw him again on May 15, 1979, and this was after a shooting incident that had occurred that involved his father, which his father apparently was shot three times, and the boy was in a marked anxiety reaction at that time, extremely tensional, and I started him on Thorazine, 10 milligrams, four times a day, because of the extreme anxiety.

Q   Immediately prior to that time when you would see him in the office what was your opinion as to the type of adjustment he was making under his new environment?

A   He was making a remarkably good adjustment. He no longer seemed as tense. He was friendly, he would go out to the front desk and talk to the girls, play with the girls. He had really made quite a remarkable adjustment.

Q   Did you then after you had seen him in May after this shooting incident to treat his anxiety created by that problem, did you see him again?

A   Yes. When his father returned home, I saw him approximately 11 days following his father's return home, because of once again major difficulties that were arising.

Q   I take it that Mrs. Wheeler was the one who brought him into the office?

A   Yes, Mrs. Wheeler brought him into the office. I had been contacted by Mrs. Wheeler by telephone on at least four or five occasions prior to this, explaining the severity of the symptoms that she felt were being suffered by the boy, and this was during the time when no one was certain whether his father was going to live or die.

Following the return home of Mr. Wheeler the boy once again was having problems because this was the second resurrection of his father, because he was finally convinced and had been prepared for the fact that his father was dead, apparently, and when his father reappeared he once again had a great shock.

Q In connection with that then did you have David come into the office and have a rather extensive consultation with David?

A Yes. I spent about an hour and a half with Mrs. Wheeler and David: about an hour with David, about half an hour getting some further history, as much as we could from Mrs. Wheeler; and he was quite free and open and spoke very freely with no difficulty.

Q When you talked with David alone what were you concerned with determining and what in fact did you learn from the boy?

A I wanted to find out as much as possible about his background first to find out whether I could determine what was causing so much of the anxiety.

What I determined from that aspect is apparently that he was very attached to his grandmother, whom he called Ma, and his grandmother died about two and a half years prior to this time, and he spoke very well of her. This was his mother's mother. He called his mother Mommy Joan, and had obviously great difficulties with her.

(I never heard David refer to his mother as "Mommy Joan." His use of this name was a contrived situation, I was convinced, as was the following information from the doctor.)

He had major fears of her. She apparently punished him for almost everything he did, and she was very strict with him. He was very frightened of her, and he was having a dream about a witch in which he kept repeating this story of an egg, which he dropped the egg, and the witch chased him with a knife into a room, and he blockaded himself in the room—apparently—I got this later from Mrs. Wheeler—apparently there was such an episode in which he dropped an egg and in which his mother ran after him, I am not sure with a knife, but that is the way he visualized it, and he locked himself in his room and would not come out for several hours, and that has become a recurrent dream with him.

The boy had developed and told me quite freely that he had developed a desire to be punished because he felt that he was to blame for many of these incidents because he was a bad boy, he would lie, and he told me so, and he would lie about anything because he was afraid to tell the truth, if he told the truth he might get punished; and this apparently related back to the circumstance with his mother originally. This is what I got from him, but yet despite this he would deliberately confront situations so as to be punished.

He spoke very freely about his grandmother, he spoke very freely about his mother in a very negative sense, but he spoke freely.

I asked him about his uncle and aunt. He refused to talk about them totally. He just stopped; he just would not speak about them.

There was an incident in which he dropped a sucker on the floor, and he became hysterical and ran to Mrs. Wheeler to get comfort and to be assured that he wouldn't be punished, and he kept saying, "I didn't mean it, I didn't mean it."

(This proved to me that David feared repercussions from Sylvi, not his mother.)

He also said that he would not call Joan his mother any more but only Sylvi—that is the present Mrs. Wheeler's first name, S-Y-L-V-I, and he was very clinging to me, and he obviously was very seeking of reassurance and comfort from a male figure.

The pattern of speech had regressed from what it had been before, and he also was clinging to his step-mother, much more than he had in prior times.

As I said, he used to just come into the office, come in, smile, exchange a few words, run out to the girls, grab a lollipop, be very friendly, come in and out. But he just clung to her as much as he could, and he did not like the idea of separation from her when we were speaking together. That is what I found out from him essentially. Then I spoke with Mrs. Wheeler, who told me that lying had become a major problem, that his behavior and his language had regressed, he had become an insomniac, she also noted that he had been very clinging and that he was now crawling along the floor the way a baby would, that he was talking to Chris on a baby level and was becoming very hyperactive and aggressive, and whenever he became agitated the infantile speech pattern became more marked.

The rest is essentially what I told Mrs. Wheeler. I told what should be done—if you want to hear that?

Q We will go into that in a minute.

When you say you asked him about his aunt and uncle and that he refused to talk about them, from your experience how do you interpret that?

A Well, it's not my experience. He said, "I don't like them. I don't want to talk about them." He just refused to have any relation to them.

After degrading Joan's relationship with her son, and writing Louise and me off David's list, Wadsworth made a thinly-disguised attempt to establish Sylvi as the savior in David's confused world.

Q At the present time who is the central figure in the boy's life?

A There is no question about that. That is his stepmother. He clings to Sylvi. He depends upon her for emotional support. He depends upon her for everything that a boy would depend on his mother for. He considers her his mother, and he told me he is no longer going to call his mother Mommy Joan, now his only mother was Sylvi.

Q And I take it that is because Mark was shot and he thought he was dead again and he was earlier told he was dead and it will take time to overcome?

A That is going to be a major problem in his life. His mother and grandmother died, his father was supposedly dead and then he reappeared and then he was shot and he was told he might die again and was apparently close to death, and the boy automatically assumed he was dead, and when the father reappeared the boy once again had a severe trauma.

People can't just keep vanishing and coming back. This is not a cartoon.

Q In your professional judgment what would be the effect if the boy was removed from the care and custody of Sylvi at the present time?

A I think it would be a disaster. She is the only person that he can cling to and have any knowledge in his own mind that she will be there, she will be steadfast, give him love and affection, she will give him attention, and she won't disappear.

Q Do you have a judgment as to whether or not the boy should be allowed to have any further contact with what is in fact his uncle and aunt, the Manns, in Salt Lake, that he apparently did not want to talk about?

A   My opinion is based on very limited access to information as to what kind of relationship they had.

He stated that he did not like them and he didn't want to talk about them, and under the circumstances at the present time I would hesitate markedly to put him into a situation where he would have contact with people whom he did not really want to have contact with.

Q   As a pediatrician I guess your main contact with the parents of any child is usually with the mother, that is the one that basically comes into the office with the children most of the time?

A   Yes.

Q   How would you evaluate Sylvi with respect to her recognizing children's problems and following instructions and carrying out the regimen that you prescribe with respect to the experience you have had with her as a mother of Christopher and David?

A   She is an extraordinarily competent and nice woman. She has great sensitivity, and she is an excellent mother to Christopher, not being overprotective, not being overbearing in any way, offering him love, security, and freedom, and she has done the same with David and she has been really his tower of strength. Without her I doubt sincerely that he would have survived.

Considering all the traumas to which he has been subjected he has done remarkably well considering the number of traumas, and I think this is really a great credit to Mrs. Wheeler.

Mrs. Wheeler has started having some doubts herself as to her capability to be able to handle all these things, and they are justifiable fears and doubts, and I have recommended to her that I thought it would be very advantageous to everybody that they enter a family counseling therapy situation with a qualified psychiatrist or psychologist so that they could all handle the situation and bring it all out.

The boy developed a peculiar reaction to his father following the shooting in that he would not admit his existence because he was afraid that he was responsible for all these things, that the boy was responsible and that if he admitted his existence again his father might once again disappear and die, and I think the nature of the circumstance is such that it would well behoove us to have some psychotherapy because of the severity of the traumas the boy has had.

He has been told his father was dead, then his father reappeared. His mother dies, his grandmother dies, his father gets shot in front of him, his best friend is not allowed to play with him any longer because of the fears on the part of the best friend's mother that her son might become involved in some violence. This is all a rather dreadful situation. If it were not for Mrs. Wheeler's remarkable capabilities I think that kid would be flying off the ceiling right now.

Wadsworth hadn't done enough to besmirch Joan. Now he pounced on the fact that she was a working mother.

Q And I suppose the fact that even before he went to live with the Wheelers, with his mother being a single lady at that time, he has not had a family relationship for some time.

Is that one of the things that he has to learn to adjust to?

A This is one of the things that I wanted to get the information about, because apparently I understand his mother was an airline stewardess and frequently would not be present. He would be left with either babysitters or relatives, his grandmother had died two and a half years before,* so he would not be with the grandmother, so all these things become very pertinent in evaluating the emotional strengths and the weaknesses of the boy.

He has been obviously in a situation where he has had to be with babysitters and/or relatives during the time his mother was working.

(*Actually, Leone had died only a year and three months earlier. The doctor was misinformed on this and other facts.)

Our attorney made a sincere attempt to refute previous implications that Joan was a neglectful mother and to establish our relationship with David. The doctor revealed that his efforts to investigate David's background were feeble, to say the least.

Q Let me follow where you left off. You talked about David having to be with relatives or babysitters.
    Do you know that for a fact?

A No, but her mother was not there. He would have to be—

Q You don't know for a fact how often his mother was or wasn't there; is that true?

A No, and that is what I am trying to find out. I asked Mrs. Wheeler to get as much information as possible. We called Dr. Lavin's office and Dr. O'Hearn's* office here, but I understand the mother lived in Denver, and we have no information as to which physician she took him to, whether the boy had any problems, or anything else.

(*The situation is ironical. Louise and I had furnished these doctors' names so that David's medical history would have continuity.)

Q As I recall you indicated you think that information is rather important; is that correct?

A Well, here is a boy who speaks of his mother in a

very negative way, and I think it would be fairly important to know whether there were any emotional crisis that had occurred before, whether or not the physician had noted anything indicating anxiety reactions before this so as to know exactly what the status was.

Q Have you ever talked with Stan Mann or his wife?

A No, I have had no contact with them.

Q Why not?

A They never called me.

Q But if you think that is important for you to know, why haven't you tried to call them?

A I didn't even know his name until this morning. I asked Mr. and Mrs. Wheeler to get as much information as they could for me, and the presumption was that they would attempt to get this, and they apparently, according to what Mrs. Wheeler told me—that their lawyer in Utah tried to get the information concerning this, but that is the only information I have.

Q As I recall, you indicated you had an hour's conference with David when he refused to talk about his aunt and uncle?

A Right.

Q Didn't you know their names at that time?

A No.

Q Why didn't you make any attempt to even find out their names?

A It really wasn't that important. I was not concerned with his aunt and uncle. I was concerned with the state of the boy, and I have been informed that he had at one time spent some time with the aunt and uncle, and so I asked him about them.

Q Do you have any idea how much time he spent with his aunt and uncle?

A None whatsoever.

Q Have you ever talked to Sylvi or Mr. Wheeler about how much time he spent with his aunt and uncle?

A I spoke with Sylvi once. She said she was not certain, she knew that he had spent some time with them but she was not very certain either, and that is where the matter dropped with trying to get the information from the physician and everything. I did not really visualize the aunt and uncle as being the center of this particular crisis.

I visualized rather the situation with the mother, the grandmother, the father as being the center of the crisis, not the aunt and uncle.

Q You indicated that the first time you knew the aunt and uncle's names was this morning?

A No. I apologize.

I believe you mentioned it yesterday afternoon? Mr. Wadsworth: Yes.

Later, our lawyer questioned the doctor about Mark's relationship with the boy.

Q Have you ever talked to Mr. Wheeler about his relationship with David?

A Yes, I have. Mr. Wheeler was present at the first conference we had in January.

Q That is just after David arrived; right?

A Yes. January 9, 1979.

Q Have you talked with him since that time?

A Yes. I spoke with him, oh, someplace in the beginning of March or April when he was with Christopher, and I asked him how things were going with David, and he said that they were going very well indeed, that everything seemed to be calmed down, that the boy was now accepting his existence and that everything was going very well.

Q   Since that time have you talked to Mr. Wheeler?

A   No, I haven't.

Q   What did Mr. Wheeler tell you in your conference in January, that is, the first conference?

A   He told me that the divorce from his first wife had been very unfriendly and that apparently his first wife had told his son, his adopted son, that he was dead; that it was very difficult for him to deal with the first Mrs. Wheeler; that she had custody of David and she just refused to allow him to see the boy.

Q   Did he indicate the last time he had seen the boy before this January situation?

A   I believe—to the best of my recollection he said he had seen him when he was someplace around one year of age.

Q   Did he indicate whether or not he had supported the boy financially?

A   No, I never asked him that.

Q   Did he talk to you about whether or not he had made any attempts to see the boy after the last time he had seen him?

A   I asked him whether he had tried, and he said the mother was very adamant and he didn't feel there should be a major confrontation, and I just dropped the subject.

Q   You didn't feel that it was important to find out his motives for seeing or not seeing the boy?

A   Well, considering the fact that the boy had been told that the father was dead I really didn't feel that Mr. Wheeler's motives in the matter really mattered.

Q   Do you think it would have made a difference to the

boy over the years had he known his father was not dead?*

A I think that would fall into the line of *res ipsa loquitur* of course.

(*David had not been told his father was dead. He thought he was a sheriff, and he had made mention of him on several occasions.)

Q If you think that is important, don't you think it is important to find out why the father did not attempt to make sure the son knew that?

A I am a physician, not a lawyer. I have to deal with facts as they are. For whatever reasons, Mr. Wheeler and his first wife had great difficulties. Mr. Wheeler said he felt it would do the boy more harm than good if he appeared, and since we have the information from the boy himself of frequent punishments for the least infraction I have the feeling, and this is just a feeling, that Mr. Wheeler felt that if he appeared the mother would punish the boy more severely for everything, that he would just aggravate the situation, and that because he did not want to do this he felt it would probably be best not to.

He made some comments about the character of the first Mrs. Wheeler and said that she was just not a very nice lady.

Now, that was his opinion.

Q Did he ever indicate that he was afraid that the boy would be punished if he tried to contact him?

A That was the impression I got. Whether he said it directly or not I really do not know.

Our attorney tried once again to establish our relationship with David. As before, the doctor's testimony was filled with false information obviously supplied by Mark and Sylvi.

Q You indicated, Dr. Marshall, I believe, that the boy's speech had regressed after he got here to California, is that right?

A   That was following the shooting.

Q   That was following the shooting?

A   Following the shooting.

Q   Was there any of this kind of regression before the shooting that you are aware of?

A   No.

Q   Did you attempt to talk to David about his aunt and uncle in January when you first saw him?

A   No. I was not aware at all of any circumstance in which the aunt and uncle would really be a major factor in the raising of the child. I did not become aware of it until later when I was informed that there was a court trial going on to determine whether or not Mark and Sylvi Wheeler would be the guardians of the child, or the custodians of the child I suppose, as opposed to the aunt and uncle.

I understood this action was brought by the uncle, and I was told that they flew to Utah, and when they came back they told me that they were the custodians of the child.

Q   Did they tell you that the child had been living with the aunt and uncle prior to that time?

A   Apparently—I don't know how long, but that he had been in their custody and living with them for some little while.

Q   You indicated that David was suffering from a separation anxiety, I think those were your words; right?

A   Right.

Q   This was in January?

A   Yes.

Q   Could this have been a separation anxiety from being separated from his aunt and uncle?

A It could have been a separation from many things, but his mother had just died and he was picked up by a father who was supposedly dead, and I believe that is enough to cause the separation anxiety.

Q Exactly what is separation anxiety?

A Essentially separation anxiety is one in which the child is afraid to leave whatever situation he is in because when he gets back he is afraid that nobody is going to be there, and that is what he was suffering from.

He was afraid to leave Mrs. Wheeler's side, Mrs. Sylvi Wheeler. He just clung to her throughout, and he was obviously very fearful that if she even walked out of the room, and she did on one occasion, she would just not come back, and he went roaring after her.

Q It was my impression that occurred after the shooting.

A No, this was in January. That is when he first came.

He was extremely anxious, and he would just not be separated from Mrs. Wheeler.

Q That is Sylvi Wheeler?

A Sylvi Wheeler, right.

Q Let me ask you. In light of your experience with David and in light of your testimony about the severe losses that he has encountered, in the event that David was attached to his aunt and uncle would the denial of his being able to talk to his aunt and uncle at this point in time add to his trauma in your opinion?

A In light of my conversations with him, he doesn't want to talk to them.

Q I think you indicated that in your conversation with him he made a statement he didn't like his aunt and uncle and didn't want to talk about them?

A Right.

Q Were there any other conversations you had with him about them?

A That was all.

Q You don't know why he didn't like them?

A I have no idea.

Q Do you know whether Mr. and Mrs. Wheeler talked about the Manns in the home?

A I think they have made every effort not to, because I asked Mrs. Wheeler about that point, and she said, "He doesn't like to talk about them and we don't talk about them."

Q If in the event he is attached to them would that harm him further, that he couldn't talk to them?

A Naturally anybody he is attached to that he could not talk to would increase the anxiety.

The final pages of the transcript merely reinforce previous testimony: that David had suffered severe shock, that he blocked out whatever he didn't want to recognize, that he had been tranquilized, and that Sylvi was his only salvation. My lawyers attempt to point out the instability of the Wheeler's marital relationship merely emphasized the doctor's determination to stress David's dependence on Sylvi.

The trial had proved one thing: Mark was not the only villain. Now Wadsworth was working in Sylvi's corner. In case of a divorce it seemed Sylvi stood a good chance of being appointed David's guardian—which meant she would try to gain control over his trust.

My ears heard the words spoken during the trial but my mind rejected the interpretation of the court. How could a judge be swayed by such distortions of fact? Surely justice would ultimately be served. Joan's last wishes could not be dismissed so easily! She had carefully prepared for David's future—all of her plans could not be destroyed!

I remembered her childhood, her growth into adolescence and young adulthood. She had always been a planner, an organizer, but her life had not always followed the route she laid out for herself. Others intervened. Interfered. Overlooked her wishes.

Just as they had now that she was dead.

Last Child of the Third Family

Joan's mother, Leone Mann, was born on January 12, 1907, the second of ten children born to George B. and Nellie Cook Mann. She was the oldest daughter and grew up in West Bountiful, Utah, working on a farm as did most of the girls in rural Utah at that time. She went on a mission for her church in 1927 and returned two years later just in time to help her mother in the care of her tenth child, Stanley Mann, and "to save him from being spoiled like the others!"

Leone and I had a special relationship. She was almost like a mother to me, this older sister of mine, and it was only natural that I should be interested in her children. Adding to this was the fact that Leone had an unusual family. At the height of the Depression, in 1934, she wed Charles Hartley, who had been married previously and had two daughters who came from California to live with their father and Leone. These girls were Betty and Virginia, and Virginia has continued to be a close friend, like another daughter to Leone, through the years.

The first child of this marriage was Gail, born in 1936, but after Leone became pregnant with the second child, her husband grew ill and passed away six weeks before his son named Charles was born in 1938. Betty and Virginia went back to California to live with grandparents, and Leone came home to live with our parents in West Bountiful. I was only eight years old, but we all went into the fields and worked, my mother and father, Leone and her children, and I. In fact, everyone worked in the fields in those days.

This was a difficult time for a woman alone with two children. No wonder she married a man 22 years older than she, a neighbor and long-time resident of West Bountiful. Charles William Newton had four children by his previous wife who had died, and his older son was only one year older than Leone. Nevertheless, C. W., as he was called, let it be known in no uncertain terms that he had little use for Leone's children. In fact, eccentric man that he was, he was very distant with his own children, who soon moved out of the house after he married again.

Joan was the second child born of this union, the first being a girl named Shauna, born in 1941, a year before Joan came along. Although much could be written about this family, Joan, in her personal journal says it with characteristic kindness:

> With my arrival on the scene, I was the last child of what remained of three families. The reason I say three is that both parents were married before—my father having four children and my mother with two. After both their spouses died, it was only natural that they should get together...which union produced my sister and myself. This permanently left me the youngest of eight children doomed to get hand-me-downs until I later leave home at the age of twenty.

There was no bitterness, no recriminations—though there were basis for both.

Of all of Leone's children, Joan was the only one who developed plumpness and skin problems. She became extremely self-conscious, and there may have been reasons for this. Charles Newton was a bitter man, one who seldom showed love or affection toward anyone. Despite this, Joan was Daddy's girl and remained devoted to her father throughout her life, though it seemed that he hardly noticed her efforts.

C. W. was a fault-finding man. He ruled his children through fear, telling them that if they would not behave, he would lock them in the basement and the "boogey man" would get them. He took great pride in the faults he could find in others, especially in Leone, her parents, and anyone else in the neighborhood his children might look up to. Joan loved her mother and her maternal grandparents who were always good to her, and this attitude of her father's must have caused her great distress because she loved him, too.

C. W.'s other children showed him little respect, and in fact he seemed to have little respect for his own father. When the old man passed away up in Canada, C. W. informed his sister that he would not go to the funeral, nor would he send flowers. "The old man never did anything for me. Why should I do anything for him?" was his final statement on the subject.

Yet this same man, without fanfare, would go to the bakery and buy bread and other food and distribute it himself to the widows in the area. I found it necessary to defend him on one occasion in front of his children who were denigrating him.—They insisted that charity should begin at home!

Because of these unhappy circumstances, all four of Leone's children took every opportunity to spend time at their Grandfather and Grandmother Mann's across the street, and probably most of their pleasant memories of childhood had their origin at that home. Shauna also gravitated to the home of my brother Charley, and Joan seemed to be attracted to our home. Louise and I treated her just like one of our own. We knew how unpleasant her own home life was at times.

Of Leone's three girls, Gail was the most attractive. She was not only beautiful, she was sweet and personable. She became very popular in high school and was elected Vice President of the student body in her senior year. Shauna was very pretty, too, but she was aloof and cold, and boys did not want to date her as she made them feel inferior. She did not want anyone to know that she was a farm girl from West Bountiful, and she went so far as to say she would never marry anyone without money, or without the potential for making big money.

Next to these beauties, Joan was just a pleasant, chubby little girl who got all the hand-me-downs. She also inherited all the jobs nobody else wanted, but she did them without complaint.

When Gail was a senior in high school, some public relations people came to the home to talk to her about becoming an airlines stewardess. Little Joan was only eleven years old, but they couldn't keep her out of the room. She listened intently to the talk about how exciting it was to be a stewardess. From that moment her career field was determined, and she worked toward that goal until she made the dream a reality.

Most things came with difficulty to Joan. She worked hard in order to accomplish things. She had to study to make good grades in school—and even then she ended up with B's and C's. Whenever anyone wanted a babysitter in the family, the job was pushed off on Joan, but she accepted her responsibility and did it with a smile. She was always appreciative and she let people around her know it, even at an early age. She was a very pleasant child.

In high school she didn't have a lot of boy friends, but she did have a lot of friends. Her sister Shauna would not even speak to her in school, wouldn't even acknowledge that Joan was her sister. This hurt Joan deeply, for she was proud of her heritage and took pride in the fact that she came from a rural background. Joan was active in pep club and other sports and extremely interested in history, world government and politics. By the time she graduated from Bountiful High School in 1960 she was 5'5", with blue eyes and blond hair, about 120 pounds, and her complexion was beginning to clear. With her pleasant smile, a permanent fixture, she was blooming into a very attractive young lady. She could hardly wait until she was old enough to become a stewardess!

The summer after she completed her junior year in high school, she worked at the Hires Root Beer stand in Bountiful. She and her friend "Cookie" came to our home one night in tears. It seems they had made the mistake of listening to some union organizers at the drive-in, as a matter of courtesy, and even though they had both informed the men they were not interested, the owner of the drive-in fired them. They needed their jobs and asked me to intervene for them. I talked the owner into reinstating the girls. After that, Joan was convinced that her Uncle Stan could do anything, and Louise and I were the ones she turned to when she needed help or advice.

Shortly after this I moved my family to Walnut Creek, California, and since Grandpa Mann had died, my mother decided to come down and live with us. Joan told us later that as she stood at the airport and waved goodbye, she felt her whole life was ending. We had been a refuge from the unpleasant conditions she had to face at home.

The next year when she graduated from high school, she came to California to visit us, and we talked to her about her plans for the future. She was not old enough, nor did she have enough business or educational experience to become a stewardess, so she decided to go to college. Because she didn't have enough money, she went to work as a bookkeeper at First Security Bank and then, having passed a civil service test, she became a clerk-typist at Hill Air Force Base. In her journal she noted:

> I recall I was extremely shocked with all the waste, laziness, bad language and worldly carrying on! Happily for me, though, the year passed quickly and in the fall I entered college.

Joan was happy at Brigham Young University and probably would have remained there except that in the summer of 1961 she met a Jim Caldwell who was home from Annapolis and provided her first real romantic fling. They carried on a correspondence to the end of the next year. It was a good thing Joan had this relationship as her mother and C. W. were divorced about this time and her Grandmother Mann died.

In the spring of 1963, Joan went to Washington, D.C., to work. Because of this move her life was to change dramatically. If she had known, would she have stayed home in Utah?

Enter: Wheeler the Dealer

Joan caught the excitement of Washington, D.C. and politics, and the coming election was too much for her to resist. She wrote:

> We went to the office of Utah's Senator Moss who found us employment in the Department of Agriculture. It was a wonderful summer of working, dating, and sightseeing .... every Tuesday all the students would go to the Washington Colosseum and hear a government speaker. This program continued throughout the summer and climaxed at the White House with President Kennedy the final speaker. It was a memorable summer but once again it was back to school.
>
> While in Washington I had met three new friends who I let talk me into transferring to the University of Utah. When I started the "U" I found the atmosphere so completely different from BYU, that it was very hard for me to adjust. The school was so cold that I didn't find it easy

to get caught up in the spirit of it all. Washington, D.C. was still beckoning to me also. I was still corresponding with friends there and since becoming more interested in politics the last few years, I really wanted to go back. With winter quarter finals over, I decided to leave school. So I packed my bags, bought my first airplane ticket (one-way), and I was off back to Washington, D.C.

Upon arriving back in Washington, my previous roommates met me and welcomed me back into the old apartment in Arlington. The first order of business was to find a job immediately on the Hill for the 1964 Presidential elections. I quickly found a secretarial job with Republican Representative John Ashbrook of Ohio for a few weeks. In the meantime I was able to secure a secretarial position with Republican Senator Everett Dirkson of Illinois. The next six months turned out to be pretty exciting for me. I was kept very busy going to one party or $1000-a-plate dinner after the next on the Hill. By this time I had fallen so in love with Washington, D.C. that I didn't think I'd ever want to leave.

It was soon after I arrived back in D.C. that I was invited out to the United States Naval Academy in Annapolis, Maryland, by a young man from my home town, to attend a weekend dance. That Sunday at church services I met a soon-to-be very special mid-shipman in my life. Mark and I were attracted to one another on first sight, I believe. The services were barely over when he walked up to me, introduced himself and right there in front of my date, slipped me a note which gave me his name, phone number and told me to give him a call if I would like a date with him! My first impressions of him were that he was good looking but extremely bad-mannered. The next thing I knew he had invited himself to lunch with us!

It was over a month before she saw Mark again, but that

was the beginning of a two-and-a-half year courtship that ultimately led to their marriage the day after he graduated.

Smitten with Mark, and certain that he held the same standards as she (after all, hadn't they met at church?), Joan decided she would now make application to the airlines, hoping that she could secure Washington, D.C. as her domicile.

She was accepted by United, her first choice. She went to Chicago for training and graduated at the head of her class, which enabled her to select Washington as her home base. She was on top of the world.

The courtship progressed, but something disturbing happened which should have been a warning to her. Mark had to go surface for duty rather than in the air where he preferred to be. Displaying the first in a series of immature acts, he pleaded with Joan to marry him, then and there, so that he would be flunked out of the Academy and not have to spend his hitch in the Navy. Joan refused to get married under the circumstances, and she continued to fly out of Washington, D.C.

Sometime in July Joan called us and asked if we were going to be in Utah for Shauna's wedding. She wanted us to meet and approve of Mark as she was getting serious about him. We told her we'd be there.

When we arrived in Utah, Leone was in a bad state. She had taken time off from work to help Shauna get ready for her wedding, and Shauna was repaying her by treating her like a maid and acting ungrateful and demanding. She even told her mother off when she couldn't take more time from work to deliver a dress for her.

Shauna had forbidden Leone to invite West Bountiful people to her wedding. Not knowing how to dress, they would be out of place, she claimed. These people were some of Leone's closest friends and she was terribly disappointed. She pleaded with Shauna, but the girl was adamant. She said

SHE would make all arrangements for her wedding! (Leone, of course, would pay for it.) On the day of the wedding Shauna was rude to her mother, ignoring both Leone and Joan, often not even introducing them to the wedding guests. Leone said it was one of the saddest experiences in her life.

For the next few days we were in Utah we had a chance to meet Mark and we were impressed with him. We both told Joan we thought it would be a good marriage. Louise later wrote Joan and told her that we were happy she had found someone special.

Mark and Joan were married at Annapolis on June 9, 1966. For several days before the wedding Joan was tempted to call it off. Her wedding outfit had been stolen and Mark's mother was giving Joan all kinds of trouble. She blamed Joan when Mark was late for a couple of ceremonies before graduation. A most outspoken woman, she delighted in making a spectacle of herself. Mark described his mother as a bigot, but there seemed to be another explanation for her action. Finally she told Joan, in no uncertain terms, that she had already picked out a girl for Mark to marry!

Whether it was his mother's attitude or some other influence, Mark was indifferent to his marriage. Besides frequent separations caused by his work, Mark seemed to have a Jekyll-Hyde personality. Joan was dumbfounded to learn he engaged in frequent drinking bouts and other activities not acceptable to their professed beliefs. Mark whitewashed his actions by saying that it was a weakness but he was going to stop it. He went on to assure her that they held the same beliefs and standards, that these were only childish things that he was going to put behind him. She had not yet disclosed her worries to us, but this must have been of extreme concern to Joan.

By this time Mark had been detailed to Long Beach, California, and Joan bid for Los Angeles as her domicile. In February, she went to her bishop, H. Whitney Chapman in

Inglewood to discuss Mark's apparent lack of interest in their marriage. Mark refused to go for any kind of counseling. They lived in Inglewood for two-and-a-half years, but Mark was home only a few months of that time. Joan felt she was lucky that they had been married quietly so that she could continue flying. (United still clung to the ruling against married stewardesses at that time.)

Mark was like a spoiled child. He barely mentioned something he wanted and Joan was expected to buy it for him. "We can't afford this," his letters read, "but IF we could...." and then he went on to describe in full detail the item he wanted. She never disappointed him. Joan was the primary wage earner. Her letters and cards are filled with references of money and gifts she sent to Mark (and very little he sent to her). Almost up to the time of their divorce she continued to be the principal breadwinner. Yet Mark was never realistic about this. When the airlines were on strike, he remarked to his parents that it was difficult when your income was cut by one-fourth. Joan's income was by far the greater of the two!

When Mark was deployed to Viet Nam, she went to visit his parents in Idaho, where she received the same cold treatment. She and Mark exchanged tapes in which they discussed certain problems, including his mother's attitude. Although Mark usually sluffed off any reference to his mother with statements like, "I don't think Mother means this," or "Sooner or later she'll come along." The tapes proved that Mark himself was the source of the problems between Joan and his mother. He had made insinuations and innuendos against Joan to his mother, by his own admissions, and that woman had believed him. Why would he speak against his own wife? Later, after we learned to know him better, we believed his action was motivated by his own insecurity, the need to be the exceptional child to his mother. He had to maintain his mother's approval at all costs, even his marriage!

Mark was in trouble career-wise, too. On August 8, 1969,

he received official notice from the Department of the Navy that his application for appointment in the navy had been turned down. With his image foremost in his mind, he could not bring himself to tell his parents. He preferred to use Joan as an excuse. He informed his folks that Joan was the thorn in his professional side; it was she who insisted he resign! Mark was a graduate of Annapolis, yet he could not even qualify for appointment in the regular navy!

Mark wasn't above asking favors of Joan, however. In August, he asked if his younger sister could come and live with Joan. She had been attending college but had gotten pregnant. It would be too embarrassing for her to return to a small town in Idaho. Could Joan take her in? He was asking for his mother, he said. Mrs. Wheeler recognized how completely unjust she had been towards Joan and could not ask her herself.

Joan took the girl in. It was not an easy situation. The girl threw wild parties and the apartment was dirty and unkempt when she returned home from flights. The girl was neither grateful nor courteous with Joan, and although she had her baby in September, neither she nor Mrs. Wheeler ever thanked Joan for what she did. Mark apologized on one of the tapes for his mother's behavior. He said he could not understand why his mother did not accept Joan.

Mark filled out resignation papers in 1970 and applied for naval reserve, for which he was also turned down. This situation seemed to substantiate the story that at one time it looked as if Mark might have been forced out of the service. In his own words he said he had "thoroughly showed up" his commanding officer in front of the men. He had demonstrated "to all of them," he said, that he was right and his commanding officer was wrong. His commanding officer's ego was such that Mark thought he might be dishonorably discharged, but the matter finally blew over.

He gave his mother another story, of course: Joan had

forced him to choose between his career and his marriage. At the time this story was being concocted, Mark was already aware that he had been turned down by the navy. He had no choice in the matter at all.

But Mrs. Wheeler called Joan and accused her of being selfish. She knew all along that Joan was not the right woman for Mark, that she would always be a hindrance to him. When Joan told Mark about their conversation, he sent back a tape saying that his mother had been wrong all along in their marriage. He labeled his mother as a "pure bigot" without question, and he could not understand why she was doing these things.

Mark resigned from the Navy on August 1, 1970, telling Joan that he was resigning because his next duty assignment would have been as advisor for one year in Viet Nam. This was an obvious fabrication.

Despite the discrepancies in his stories, Joan looked forward to civilian life and the hope that they would adjust to one another now that Mark was home for good. Her hopes were shortlived. The service hadn't been their problem. Mark was their problem, and this problem was only compounded when he left the navy.

Civilian Life with a Con Artist

With Mark out of the service Joan envisioned a normal family life and children in the near future. But Mark didn't know what he wanted to do. They decided that Joan would continue to work for two more years while he went to San Diego State to get an MBA. They financed a little home through VA and moved in. Joan fixed up the yard and added homey touches and Mark went to school while she continued to fly out of Los Angeles.

After his first year of studies—and a trip to the Orient on a free ticket—Mark decided he did not want to return to school. He was hired for a job with Electronic Data Systems and off he went to New York. They were separated for a few months until Joan could sell the house in California, and then she joined him and they bought another home, this time in Matawan, New Jersey. Transferring with United, she flew out of Newark International Airport, and they settled in, after ten months, when Mark announced that he was required to attend a computer school in Dallas, Texas. Joan stayed behind to tend the house and soon learned that he had been transferred, "temporarily," to L.A. She flew out as often as she could, but it wasn't until spring that she learned this was a permanent transfer. She sold their New Jersey home and moved to California where she bought a beautiful house in Woodland Hills.

Their unsettled state paralleled their emotional life. Even before he left for computer school, Mark became increasingly preoccupied. He spent considerable time away from home, even on weekends. The marriage relationship was such that Joan asked Mark if there were anyone else. He responded, "No comment." (At a later time Mark admitted that he had been seeing other women, but that he had not lied to her—he had simply not answered.)

Mark had a friend named Bill Curley with whom he said he spent his weekends and when Mark left for computer school, he turned his house key over to Bill. Bill used their house all summer and into the fall during Joan's absences, and when she returned from her flights, Bill attempted to take over Mark's place in the household. Joan was shocked. She called Mark in Dallas and told him what Bill was trying to do. His response was, "So what? I'm busy. I don't have time to discuss it."

Joan didn't want Mark to accept even a temporary job in L.A., but she decided she would try to make a go of it. They applied at an adoption agency to see if they could get a baby and Joan went to L.A. to spend some time with Mark, hoping to heal the breach. She took a cab to Mark's apartment and found a letter on the table from a Mrs. G. T. from Idaho. When Mark arrived home, she asked him about it. He was evasive. And he also refused to talk about his mother's attitude or Bill Curley. Joan was fed up. She had taken all she could, and there seemed to be no solution. She thought it best if they separated. Now Mark, who had previously been adamant about no counseling or even a discussion of their problems with anyone, suggested that they go to talk with a bishop.

They went to the Wilshire Ward and met with Bishop Ensign B. Call. Bishop Call told Mark that he had to get his priorities straight, that he should set his mother right, and furthermore, he asked him if he had had an affair with this woman in Idaho. Mark denied that there had been. He said he was trying to help an old friend solve her marital problems! The bishop talked to each of them separately and asked Joan if she thought Mark was a homosexual or bi-sexual. She had never thought of this. She was shocked. (Months later she found out that when Bishop Call had asked Mark the same question, he had looked at the ceiling and refused to answer.)

Joan had to return to New Jersey to sell their house, and Mark agreed to talk with Bishop Call again. He never got around to it, however, and later when Joan asked him to go with her, he refused.

Mark's assignment at EDS was as a management consultant with Goldstein Samuelson in Beverly Hills. He was privileged to have access to their financial data wlich was quite confidential and extremely detailed. While working here, Mark opened an account for purchasing commodity options, and on February 6th, he bought six double options of September 1973 coffee futures and the next day he bought seven double options for September 1973 plywood. Both of these purchases were made on margin as Mark had no money to invest and obviously no idea how he would pay for them. The day after the purchase, the options started to decline. By February 9th he could see that he was in a tight spot.

He called Joan, told her he had a friend in the "know," and they could make a lot of money if they were to buy the options. Maybe her mother might want to invest and get in on the action. On February 10th, Leone loaned Mark $4,500 which he was going to invest "in the futures." At the same time he called an old school friend from Rupert, Idaho, now living in L.A., and he got $2500 from Paul and MarJean Lewis. On February 15th, James Coleman, a classmate of Mark's at Annapolis, gave him $1250 for the same purpose. James was in land development in California. (Later he was indicted for land fraud)

Somehow, probably through the use of the computer he was working on, Mark delayed the printing of an invoice that divulged the purchase of these options until February 19th. He was working on Goldstein Samuelson's money! On February 22nd, he paid the amount he was required to put up for the margins, ($6,696.00) and the remaining $1,554.00 he kept in his own personal account. He put no money of his own into the investment, nor did he return any of the excess amount to the investors or repay their original investment. He arranged for the check which he paid to be withdrawn from the domestic account and placed in another account—the international account—of Goldstein Samuelson while still showing payment on the purchase of options under his name.

Just five weeks after these transactions, Goldstein Samuelson Inc. declared bankruptcy. His procedures in depositing the check and the adjustment of the deposit, along with several other steps, Mark had written on the back of his customer acknowledgement of his purchase, in his own handwriting.

The same week the bankruptcy occurred, Mark returned to New Jersey to help Joan move some of their possessions out to California. As far as Joan knew, everything was fine. When they were about ready to leave—the movers had picked up their furniture and they were to embark on a new life together—Joan and Mark came to my office to say goodbye. Mark was his typical self. I noticed no change in his behavior, nor any indication that there might be a problem. I was living at the Essex House in NYC while we were building a house in Short Hills, New Jersey, and Louise was with me. The children were with friends at our old home in Northbrook, Illinois.

Leone, Joan and Mark were on their way out to California and would be stopping to rest at our home the next morning. Everything seemed fine. They went on their way.

Joan filled me in on the details later. There was no indication of a problem until they arrived at the outskirts of Chicago. At this time, Mark pulled off the interstate highway and into the parking lot of the Holiday Inn near O'Hare International Airport. After he had parked, Mark turned to her and said, right in front of Leone, "Joan, I don't love you any more. I think I want out." There was no further explanation. He simply wanted her to take him to the airport so he could fly out to California. She could continue to drive but she was not, under any circumstances, to tell anyone what had happened.

Joan was in shock. What *had* happened? She had no warning, no premonition even, and she didn't know what to think. She came to when Mark demanded the $8,000.00 check which they had received for the sale of their New Jersey home. What was he saying? Did he want to leave her destitute? She pulled herself up short and refused. He insisted. When she refused again, he threw himself into a rage. She endorsed the back of the check, but shrewdly she signed it over to the escrow company in L.A. where they were purchasing another home.

Mark threw such a tantrum when he saw what she had done that she jumped back into the car and took off with her mother for our home in Northbrook. The next day they left and drove straight through to Salt Lake City.

Joan laid low for a few days at her mother's house in Bountiful and tried to work things out in her mind. She was exhausted, both mentally and physically, and didn't want to worry her mother about her trouble. But she needed to talk to someone. Fortunately, she learned that Bishop Call from

California was in town for April Conference, and he was staying with some of his family who lived in Bountiful. Joan called him and he rushed right over to her mother's home. He advised Joan to divorce Mark. He could see no solution to his problems, since he wouldn't work on them.

Joan went on to L.A. to the new home. She finally called me and told me what had happened. She asked for my counsel but told me she still loved Mark. What was I to tell her? I wanted her happiness. I thought perhaps they could work it out. After all, at that time I had no idea of Mark's involvement. After our talk she decided she would call Mark at his apartment and tell him she still loved him and would give him thirty days to make up his mind.

After two weeks she had still heard nothing from him. She called Mrs. Wheeler who said Mark was there at the time, but she felt Joan was the cause of all their problems because she looked down on farmers. This was a surprise to Joan, as she had always been proud of her rural heritage. Mark had always been the one apologetic about his background. He made frequent references to "dumb farmers."

The following Sunday, when she figured Mark would be back at his apartment, she called and told him that she couldn't wait any longer for his decision. In light of what his mother had said, she was going to file for divorce. Completely out of the blue, Mark said he wanted to come home and be a full-time husband. He said he had gone to Idaho to see an Elder Griffin for advice. But he gave no further explanation—and she didn't see him for another two weeks! Finally, out of desperation she called this Elder Griffin and he said that he hadn't seen Mark in years. On impulse, Joan telephoned Mrs. T. who admitted that Mark had been with her. They were in love and had been for five years, she said. Joan offered to divorce Mark, but Mrs. T. said she decided that she was in love with her husband after all. Mark had lied to her, too! She also disclosed that Mrs. Wheeler had known about their relationship all along. Mrs. T. had been Mark's confidante all the years he was in the navy and he wrote to her about his drinking parties and the fact that he was currently stepping out with a Kathryn Parker of Downey, California. Furthermore, she revealed that she and Mark usually met at the home of Mark's sister, the sister that Joan had taken into her home when she was pregnant and unmarried.

Mark didn't deny it. He said he was in love with both of them but his marriage was precious to him and he wanted her to go to counseling with him. She couldn't refuse to go since this is what she had wanted for so long. They started on a course of counseling during which time Mark continued to see Mrs. Parker and to drink with his buddies and neighborhood friends behind her back.

Meanwhile Mark raved to Margaret Keller at LDS Social Services about the solidarity of their marriage. He had everyone, including Joan, convinced they were completely in love and that their home would be a perfect place to raise a child.

Joan continued to be the chief wage earner and to center her interests in her home and church work. Sometimes she was discouraged but Mark seemed to be doing better and maybe all of their differences would be resolved if they had a baby. After all, there is no more positive hope for the future than a young child to build your plans around. Besides, she had always longed for a child and Mark seemed to want one, too. Look how he talked to Mrs. Keller.

She began to relax and pray that she might be able, one day, to stay home and be a homemaker and mother.

A Heavy Family Man

Up to this point I hadn't known a lot about the difficulties that Joan was undergoing. But suddenly everything seemed to fall into place—and I was there when they did.

In January of 1974, Mark quit EDS and began commuting to Salt Lake City to work for Lund and Company. Joan did not move to Salt Lake City, fortunately enough, for the company went under just six months later, but Mark was sure he'd found the right field. This was what he'd been looking for all along. He could make some real money here. I had heard that story before—and I would hear it again.

I was in Salt Lake to give a talk to the business school at Brigham Young University and thought I'd spend a few extra days and get in some skiing. I met Mark at Shauna's. He started to tell me all about the new company that had been organized by a group of young tigers—of which he was one, a leader, in fact—and their novel approach of using other people's money to make fast money for themselves. This was the thing for him. No more working in a company where it took years to go up the hard way. No, sir, here he had a chance for instant success. He would get into the big time overnight. It was like the knights of old, going out to slay their dragons instead of waiting at home for things to come to them, "like some dumb old farmer."

Just the day before, I had dinner at a little Mexican restaurant in Salt Lake where I heard a familiar voice in the next booth. Leaning back I could see that it was Mark, as I suspected, with a young lady—and the customary brown bag, a common sight with those who drink alcoholic beverages in Utah. It was the first time I had encountered his split personality but when I saw him the day after, at Shauna's, suddenly everything started to fit together.

A couple of months after his conversation about getting ahead fast, the Lund Company went broke and Mark went without work for several months. Sometime in September, with the help of a friend, he was able to get work with Touche Ross in Los Angeles.

We didn't see Joan and Mark again until Christmas of that year, and I put aside my reservations because everything seemed fine. We were all at my sister Leone's place. Mark was interested in his job and told me some of the assignments he was working on.

My red flag went up again though when he inquired, "Stan, how do you pick the faction that is going to win in a business?" I asked him to explain what he meant. He elaborated. "You know, which side will be the power group, the 'in' group?"

My suspicions were up, but to give him the benefit of the doubt, I asked casually, "Explain that again. I'm not sure I understand." Possibly I had misunderstood him.

I hadn't. He repeated the same idea. He was completely serious.

I tried to explain to him that I had not picked a particular faction. I tried to understand my responsibilities and what I was accountable for and then did the best I could. As my superior moved up in the corporation, openings developed either through his moving up, or through growth in the company. There was never any faction to be "in" with.

He still persisted. "But how can you pick the ones going up and how can you get attached to them?"

"The operations I have worked in have been extremely successful, Mark, but I haven't found this kind of situation there."

He looked disappointed. "That is very unusual. A rare situation, because getting with the right group is the way it is done 99% of the time."

He was convinced of it!

Several days later Leone disclosed to me that she had overheard the discussion and she was bothered about it. He seemed to think that he could gamble and show very little responsibility and let Joan work to pay the bills. He had been at Touche Ross a short time and advancement was much too slow for him, he felt. Leone said this was a matter of disagreement between Mark and Joan on several occasions.

Joan did not want to work all her life. She wanted children. She wanted to be a mother and a homemaker. If he kept moving from one job to another, rather than trying to develop some sort of security, she might have to quit work and let him foot the bills. Mark responded savagely. "I am the man of the house. I make the decisions, and if you try to tell me what to do, I'll see you on a slab!"

Leone was aghast when she heard this, but Joan later told her that Mark threatened her life on more than one occasion when she didn't go along with his ideas.

In the middle of March I became more involved in their lives. Joan called me on a layover in New York and asked if I would meet her. I did. She was very upset. She proceeded to tell me some of the problems they had. Mark could be charming when other people were around, but when they were alone, he was extremely moody, with periods of deep depression, mainly over his feelings that he wasn't getting ahead as fast as he felt he deserved. When he was depressed, he would go to the military dispensary and get large amounts of drugs, both "uppers" and "downers." Joan took calls from both work and church about assignments he was supposed to have completed and hadn't. There were meetings he hadn't shown up for, when in fact he had left the house headed for those appointments.

Then she showed me the book recording the transactions at the time he purchased the "futures" contract. She asked me what I thought she should do, knowing that he had stolen money from his friends and from her mother. He has used this money, she said, but couldn't account for it, and he had threatened her life if she said anything about it.

It was not an idle threat. She had reason to fear for her life. She showed me a Master Charge purchase slip that proved on February 7, 1975, just a few weeks before, at the Bell Jewelry and Loan Company in Phoenix, Arizona, he had purchased a PPK/S Walther Automatic, under the name of John Paris Oberhansly whose address was listed as 1225 East University #19. Joan further said that he had two other hand guns that she was aware of, that were not registered to him. This was the first time she had known him to buy a gun under a false name and address.

I was dumbfounded. He was a felon on top of everything else. To buy time, I asked her how everything seemed to be going. To my surprise she answered that, despite these matters, things were fairly good. However, she felt very nervous because he had threatened her life and things like this gun purchase upset her.

She went on to say that she had heard him lie to someone on the telephone one time and when she asked him about it, he threatened her life and told her it was not a woman's position to question her husband, and that no real man would ever let a woman do it. He never raised his voice. He didn't seem to be angry, but she knew he meant it. Yet when they went out with friends, he was Mr. Personality.

Joan longed for a child. She had prayed about it for many years and finally she asked Mark to fast and pray with her on the subject. He refused, said he didn't believe in fasting. The only thing it did for him was to make him hungry.

Nevertheless, on April 10, 1975, Joan and Mark got a beautiful baby boy, whom they named David, from LDS Social Services. Things were better between Mark's parents and Joan, and Mark admitted to the Social Services counselor, Brother Craner, that he, himself, had been to blame for these misunderstandings. Things seemed greatly improved. Joan was still working, but she spent as much time as she could with the baby and took delight in the family the three of them had become. Mark would not hear of her quitting work, so she continued to fly out of Los Angeles.

In October Mark was put on assignment to Schick Sunn Classic Productions, Inc. He began telling Joan some of the usual office stories. One was about the affair between the President of Sunn Classics and his secretary, a Miss Sylvi Ingebrigtsen. In fact, after Mark had worked there for a while, he told Joan this Sylvi was carrying on with several other executives at Sunn Classics as well.

In mid-November, Mark became very quiet about his work. He quit discussing things at Sunn Classics with Joan. He started to work long hours and came home only to sleep, sometimes only for one or two hours a night. He took stimulants to keep himself going, and he said he was traveling to Denver and Dallas on business trips for the firm.

The time was fast approaching when they would sign the final adoption papers for David. As soon as they were signed, Joan was planning to ask Mark again if she could resign her position with United Airlines and stay home and be a full-time mother. Mark's income, for the first time in their marriage, would approximate Joan's and they should be able to handle their bills on his salary. They had paid off all of their bills except the house, and she was sure they could make it. At the back of her mind was a small worry because Mark was not picking up the baby at the sitter's when he was supposed to. Sometimes he was four or five hours late. If she were not working, the responsibility for the bills might make Mark a little more stable.

Two days before Thanksgiving Mark instigated a call to Social Services and raved about how great their home was now that David was with them. However, he told Joan he was pressed to get some work finished and that he would have to work all during the holidays. He wouldn't have even a single day off.

"Why don't you take David and go spend the Christmas holidays with your family? Then I can spend all my time on work and get caught up. There is no way I can be with you, anyway."

When he told this, on December 5th as Joan took her mother to the airport to return home after a visit, Joan said she would probably be in Salt Lake for the holidays. However, she would make her final decision after Mark rested up over the week-end. Mark had been very cold again for several weeks but she hoped to be able to talk to him. He was exhausted, she knew, because he never played with David. The only time he seemed to notice the baby was when someone else was around. When they were alone, he was always too tired.

She never had a chance to talk to him. He was moody the entire week-end and when Monday came, he packed his bags and said he had to take a trip to Denver and would be gone all week. This was a surprise to her. She had scheduled only two days of flying in December, according to Mark's previous plans, because she didn't know he was to be gone. Early on Tuesday evening someone from Mark's office called to talk to him. Joan said that Mark was not there—Was there a message, she asked? The caller answered, "Never mind the message. I'll talk with him at the office tomorrow morning." The next day Joan called and asked for Mr. Wheeler at the office. They said that he was out at that time but would be returning before the day was over. Needless to say, she was confused.

On Wednesday evening Mark called her. He asked how things were and said he had been so tied up in Denver that he hadn't been able to spend any time in his hotel. He also mentioned how cold it was. He had to stay indoors because he didn't have a heavy topcoat for that kind of weather. Joan asked him if it had been snowing there in Denver. He answered, "Yes. Most of the day." Then he told her again how sorry he was about the holidays and about her going to her mother's without him. She let him continue. He was obviously enjoying himself.

After hanging up, she sat for hours trying to analyze the situation and figure out why he was lying to her. Just a few weeks before, they had their final interview on the adoption and Mark had gone out of his way to tell Margaret Keller how happy they were and how perfect everything was in their home. Joan felt she was living on a roller coaster. To their church friends Mark was a perfect husband and father. He told everyone how devoted he was and they believed him. But at home, alone with Joan and David, he was a moody, beleaguered man, an habitual liar given to making threats on her life. So far he had not really mistreated David, but what would be next? She honestly didn't know. He seemed capable of anything. She knew there were no limits to his ambition. He would take whatever steps he thought would put him in the front line for advancement. Why draw the line at anything else?

Suddenly her body was shaken by a chill. What kind of man had she married? She felt betrayed and demoralized. As if he knew his mother's thoughts were centered on him,

David stirred and whimpered in his sleep. Quickly Joan picked him up, comforting him in her shaking arms. She spent the rest of the night holding the boy, trying to sort out their position in this crazy kaleidoscope that Mark had placed them in.

David, Child of Love

Document #104-75-064646, labeled Certificate of Live Birth, the State of California—Department of Health, dated January 12, 1976, lists David Mark Newton Wheeler as the child of Joan Newton and Mark Wayne Wheeler, residence Woodland Hills, Los Angeles County, California. The child's birthdate is listed as March 12, 1975, and states "Record Amended January 9, 1976."

Those are the statistics in David's young life. They do not tell the story, only the facts of his adoption.

No child was ever more dearly longed for, more keenly anticipated. Joan had wanted a child for years. She had collected a dresser full of baby clothes a year before David came to her. Her greatest desire in life was to be a full-time wife and mother. She did not resent working—she loved her position as flight attendant—but she felt she had a higher calling, and she was eager to get on with it.

Even after they took David into their home, Mark would not let Joan resign her position with United, but she' did the next best thing. She spent all of her off-duty time with the boy, and managed to give him a rich, full home life in spite of his father's absences.

No home was ever more child-centered. Joan not only bought everything that David needed to provide a good wholesome growing environment, she also added extra incentives. On the walls, as David grew up, were charts and reminders for him to brush his teeth, pick up his toys, to do other chores in keeping with his level of development. He was reminded gently to say his prayers and to be kind to his playmates. All of these posters bore drawings and cartoons which Joan herself had devised, complete with splashes of reds, yellows and blues so attractive to youngsters.

David went first class. His Halloween costumes were handmade, with details appropriate for the finest custom tailoring: finished seams, innerlined facings, meticulous trimmings. One year he delighted in being a clown. The next, a mouse with head gear complete with stand-up ears. Joan had been called to work before she finished his Christmas stocking that last year, but no child ever looked forward to picking Christmas goodies out of the depths of a more ornate stocking.

These were typical of the care and attention Joan gave to the welfare of her little son. Pasted in a scrapbook was a card given to David on his first birthday. "To David, my son, with love on his first birthday." This $25 check will start your missionary fund. Love, Mother." David's favorite song was "I Hope They Call Me On A Mission," a tune he sang at full volume at the drop of a hat when he was three years old. And he made frequent mention of things he would need when he went on his mission—"a car, some new clothes...." Joan was making plans for the time, years in the future, when David would be eligible to go on a mission for his church.

David was an adopted child—and for some time, a one-parent child—but he never suffered from lack of love or attention. In the book of momentos Joan collected is a letter from his substitute mother for one month.

Dear Mama and Daddy,

Here's your little Saturday Warrior! And he is, too!!

A sweet and cuddly baby that loves to be held—yes, we've spoiled him, but he got lots of love.

Let me give you his daily schedule.

Wakes between 5 and 6 am and has 5 oz. of Enfamil (which includes 1 oz. of Pet canned milk) warmed. Goes back to sleep for an hour or so—wakes and is turned to tummy and sleeps for another hour or so.

About 9:30 I give him a sponge bath—and get him dressed for the day. I notice he has a tendency for cold feet so I usually keep him in booties.

Has 5 oz. of Enfamil (with Pet). Is awake till next feeding—just cat naps. Likes to sit in infant seat—lay on sofa and to be held. Travels well—I usually run my errands or whatever now.

At 1:30 or 2 has another 5 oz. and goes to sleep till around 6 and has another 5 oz.

Is awake in evening. Cat naps. At 9:30 or so I give him his bath. Likes it till all his clothes come off and then he really cries. After I take him out of the water I wrap him in his towel and hug him. Gets in night clothes. I only use Baby Lotion on him.

Another 7 oz. of formula—I had him to doctor Tuesday and he suggested cereal. He's had it twice 2 T rice cereal with part of formula. LOVES IT!

I give it to him before his bottle. Takes almost all of milk —but doesn't go to sleep. This is his STINKER time. HE LOVES HIS BINKY! Wants to be rocked. Takes rest of milk and finally settles down between 11:30 and 12 and then sleeps through.

Has one or two BM during day. Usually while taking a

bottle. I wash bottles in hot water and rinse well. Wash nipples and caps and bring to boil for a couple of minutes. Make up bottles as needed. I've washed his clothes in White King and he seems to have no problems. Sleeps mostly on sides, sometimes on tummy.

Here's a picture at 5 days and I have more in camera—I'll see that they are sent on to you.

INFO FOR BABY BOOK
Weighed 9 lbs 5 oz. at birth.
2 days 9 lbs 1 oz.
1 week 9 lbs 12 oz.
2 weeks 10 lbs 12 oz.
3 weeks 11 lbs
4 weeks (yesterday) 11 lbs. 12 oz. This is on my scale with stretch suit on.

Penis healed at 7 days. Cord came off at 12 days.

Tear ducts do not function properly. Doctor said not to worry. Eyes get matted. Wash with boric acid solution.

Is hard to burp. Try during bottle. Hold high on shoulder or try sitting on lap, cupping chin with hand and patting with other. Sometimes will not at all. Will kind of squirm when ready to burp. If he gets a tummy ache, put your hand on his tummy, the warmth seems to help. Doesn't have them often.

May God bless you all.

In addition to showering David with love and care, Joan bore another burden. She felt duty-bound to the child's biological parents. It was they who had provided a child for her. They had entrusted their dear baby into her keeping, and as with everything else she undertook, she intended to do an exceptional job of rearing him. Many times, because of Mark's irresponsibility, she felt she had let the boy's natural parents down because she could not provide a two-parent home as they wished for David.

The agency told Joan about David's natural parents. They were both attending a local university in Southern California, probably the University of Southern California or UCLA, and the father was on an athletic scholarship, for football, as I recall. After forty-one weeks of gestation labor began, lasting eight hours and 27 minutes, and on Wednesday, March 12, 1975, at 1:24 P.M. this co-ed gave birth to a robust baby boy weighing nine pounds and five ounces. The baby was 21 inches in length, his head measured 15 inches and his shoulders spanned 16 inches. His blood type, RH Positive, matched his mothers. Although delivery was spontaneous, the doctor, Dr. Charles S. Brolerg, used a spinal anesthesia and mid forceps. The birth took place at Huntington Memorial Hospital in Pasadena, California.

Twenty-eight days later, on April 10, at 1:00 P.M., Brother Craner, head of Social Services, and Margaret Keller presented that beautiful baby boy to Joan and Mark at LDS Social Services, 1989 Riverside Drive, L.A., with all the expectations that any agency has when placing an adoptive child in a home. That Thursday was the greatest day in Joan's life, and it seems certain that Brother Craner and Margaret Keller were sincere in their thinking. But, unfortunately, one of the adults present was not sincere. He had schemed for months, probably years, and was not about to let himself be drawn into responsibility of this sort. Joan had tried to overlook Mark's past actions, to let herself believe that he wanted a child as much as she did, and he played a good part, even calling the social services office and raving about how happy he and Joan were and what a good home they would provide for a baby.

Sincerity was not in Mark's make-up. At the same time as he pronounced these feelings, he was already involved with another woman and making plans to leave Joan. Within one hour after the adoption was final, Mark would take Joan and

David home from the courthouse and leave the household permanently. He didn't have time for them anymore, he stated, and he could not tie up his money with them as he had to think of his future family.

In view of Mark's default, Joan felt a keen sense of responsibility for the boy in addition to her love for him because his natural parents had given David to her to raise. She loved him selflessly and sacrificed for him like no one else could have.

David was a big, strong, extremely active boy right from the start. He grew at a rapid rate, and when Joan left on her last flight, she took with her a suitcase full of Christmas clothing purchased in November, which had to be exchanged because it was too small.

His adoptive father never took much interest in him but after he left the home, he neglected David shamefully. Before Joan's accident he had failed to contact the boy or to pay child support for twenty-two months! But immediately at Joan's death he seemed to reverse his attitude and suddenly he played the concerned parent. Obviously David's trust was the motivation.

I took an oath to keep this trust out of Mark's hands. The child was wrested from my home, and Mark and his attorneys have made every effort to break the trust, but so far they have not been successful. I swore to Joan that if I could not fulfill the requests made in her will and trust, that I would make every effort to find David's natural parents, with the hope that they may have married, or if not, that one of them would see the desperate need David has for them to step forward and claim him at this time.

Mark has admitted twice under oath that he left home and was not living with Joan at the time of the adoption. Under the circumstances, any reasonable court in the land would award David to his natural parents if they were to seek custody, and no boy ever needed the love of his parents more than David. At the present time he is kept under tranquilization and isolated from friends and relatives. He is a pawn in a battle for personal gain by a man who is completely unscrupulous about anyone who gets in his way. He does not care about David. He did not care about Joan. He cares only about Mark Wheeler.

Every child has a right to mature parents who love and protect him. Children need our protection. My heart breaks when I think of David, alone, bewildered, fearful. But the court has decreed that I cannot take care of him. He needs his natural parents, he needs them desperately, and if they will contact me, I will handle their inquiries with complete confidentiality, according to their wishes.

David is a special child, bright, alert, and inquisitive.— A lovable little boy with the energy of a dynamo, the creativity of an inventor, and the soul of a poet. Anyone claiming him would gain a gem of inestimable value.

As a little boy David seemed to have everything in the world going for him—except a daddy. His natural father, for reasons best known only to him, could not raise him. His adoptive father couldn't be bothered with him, that is, not until after Joan's death when he thought David's trust would put him on easy street for the rest of his life.

I cannot believe that Mark has one shred of love or concern for David's well-being. Nothing in his past points in this direction, and all of his previous actions seem to indicate that Mark is, again, out for a killing without much effort. At David's expense.

The Great Cover-Up

Joan had asked her mother to come back to take care of David while she worked those two flights just before Christmas 1975. Mark seemed to be pleased about the arrangements because Joan would have someone to drive to Utah with.

Nothing was said about the so-called phone calls from Denver and Mark left for work. About four o'clock that afternoon, he telephoned and said he had to work with a friend on the computer at Itell Corporation. He would not be home until very late.

Joan got David ready for bed and she and her mother sat in the living room talking over her problems with Mark. They thought David was settled for the night, but sometime later when Joan went in to check on him, he had crawled into the guest room looking for "Ma" and when Joan found him, he had ingested the entire contents of a bottle of her mother's high blood pressure pills.

Frantically, Joan called to her mother. Leone confirmed that the bottle had been almost half full. On the telephone the pediatrician advised Joan to rush David to the hospital. He would meet her there. They arrived about 9:15 P.M. and the doctor started treating David immediately.

Joan tried to call Mark at Itell; however, the night man said no one was in the computer time rental room. Joan called a friend of Mark's from church and he tried to get in touch with Mark. No success.

After pumping David's stomach and medicating him, they sent Joan and the patient home about midnight. Joan had not been well and had missed sleep for several days so her mother offered to watch David while Joan caught up on a little rest. Relieved, Joan went to bed about 2 A.M.

About 2:30 Mark staggered in. It was apparent he had been drinking.

Joan roused herself. "Mark, where have you been?"

"Been?" he answered defensively. "I've been at Itell, using the computers."

Joan steeled herself. "We've been calling there since shortly after ten o'clock. The man on duty said no one had been there from ten o'clock on." She paused and swallowed hard several times. "Mark, where *have* you been?"

"That guy was mistaken. I was there all along. It happens all the time. They're too lazy to go back and check." He pulled off his coat and tie. His tone was abusive. "Why do you try to check up on me, anyway? Don't bother me when I'm trying to work, do you understand? Leave me alone!"

She held back the tears that started to well up, unbidden, in her eyes. "Mark, I wasn't trying to check up on you. I needed you desperately. David...David had an accident. I had to take him to the hospital."

"Hah!" he scoffed. "D'you 'spect me to fall for that hogwash? C'mere, give me a little lovin'. That'll straighten you out, baby."

"Mark, no, please no." She recoiled from his touch.

"That's typical of all you women. You all want it but

won't admit it. A good roll in the hay will fix you up, kid."

Joan tried to resist, but in spite of her protests, Mark proceeded to assault her, both physically and sexually.

She had never felt so degraded in her life. Mark was using stimulants to keep him going and awake, and she tried to attribute his strange behavior to narcotics, but that didn't soften the sting of his treatment.

After only four hours sleep, he left the next morning and told her that since he would be working late again, he would get a room at a motel near the office. "I'll grab a few hours sleep and get right back to work. Don't bother me again at work, Joan. Do you understand? Don't bother me."

"We have an appointment on Friday morning to sign the final adoption papers for David," she reminded him.

"Don't worry. I'll be there," he flung behind him as he slammed the door on his way out.

The next few days were hell for Joan. On Thursday evening Mark called and said he had been staying at a motel—he refused to tell her which one—but he told her to be ready the next morning as he planned to pick her and David up to go to the courthouse.

The next day they drove from their home in Woodland Hills to the Los Angeles County Courthouse in downtown L.A. Just before they entered Room 217 where they were to meet the lawyer and the judge, Mark said to Joan, "Relax. Don't look so tense. They are not going to know a thing."

Joan frowned. "What do you mean?"

"They won't know I'm not living with you."

Joan went through the ceremony in a trance. She felt as if she weren't even there. She seemed to be standing over her own body and observing this hoax which was taking place. A loving couple taking an innocent child into their home. What a farce!

After they had signed the papers, Mark took them directly home, reached over in front of her to open the door, and told her clearly that he did not have time for her any more. "Adopting a baby does not save a bad marriage, Joan."

"Oh, Mark, do you know what you're doing? Come in. Maybe we can talk out our problems—or at least find out what they are!"

"Forget it, Joan. I'm through." And he drove off.

Joan watched his car pull off just as the mailman delivered their mail. With David in her arms, she emptied the box and went into the house, her heart in her throat and her brain teeming in confusion. Was she going mad? Did she imagine all these lies that Mark told her? Was she wrong about him?

By habit she started opening the letters in her hand. There was one from Itell Corporation.—A billing for computer time that Mark had used. She followed down the sheet with her finger. Monday, December 15th. Clocked in at 7:04 P.M. Clocked out at 8:06 P.M. One hour and two minutes! The night that Mark claimed he had worked until 2 A.M. The night David had been rushed to the hospital. The night Mark had assaulted her. "Oh, why, Mark? Why?"

Joan called Bishop T. Curtis Price, Woodland Hills III Ward, and he responded to her call immediately. She contacted Mark's boss who confirmed that Mark had been in L.A. the whole time he said he was in Denver. Bishop Price contacted Mark at work to try to make appointments with him, but Mark broke all three appointments. The last appointment was on December 30th, at 10:00 P.M. Mark later told the Bishop that he was at work until very late and his Porsche was stolen. Under all the pressure he didn't have time to call. Joan and her mother happened to drive by the place where Mark was supposed to be working on that particular night and no one was there!

But on January 3rd, Mark finally popped in on the Bishop. He refused to tell the Bishop where he was staying, told him he would not face Joan, but informed him that he wanted a divorce. The Bishop should tell her just that.

The Bishop dutifully delivered Mark's message and Joan had divorce papers served on him January 7th. Mark refused all counseling from both church and the county. (When Joan's brother, Charley, from Colorado Springs, visited Mark the previous November, he was repulsed by his filthy language and his bragging about all the drinking he was doing on the road. Mark had just been called to a stake mission for his church! There were many rumors at this time about his drinking and going to topless and bottomless bars, and he had been reported to the Bishop.)

Thirty minutes before the divorce papers were served on Mark, Joan talked to him on the telephone. Immediately after the papers were served on him, he called her back.

"Why couldn't you wait? The papers make it so final. If you'd just wait a while—let me get my head on straight—I might want to come back."

Joan couldn't believe her ears. It was he who had insisted on the divorce.

At the hearing on January 28th, Mark refused to give any support or assistance, saying, "I can't tie up my money with David. I have to think of my future family."

What was he saying? His future family? During the years preceeding their adoption of David, Joan had undergone extensive tests to determine the reason she couldn't conceive. Finally, after some time, Mark had a sperm test which determined that the problem was his. Nothing was wrong with her. It was Mark.—His future family? Under the circumstances it seemed highly unlikely that he was talking about an adoptive family. What on earth, then, did he mean?

The Manipulator Revealed

Later we were to learn, Joan and I, that on March 28th, Mark and Sylvi purchased a home to be built. Mark denied under oath, later admitted under oath, and then again denied, still under oath, the existence of this property and his ownership.

During all the legal entanglements, we learned something about Mark: he was the fastest perjuror in the West! The truth meant nothing to him. As long as he stood to gain from a lie, he perjured himself over and over. Lying was as natural as breathing to him.

The day after Mark and Sylvi purchased their home, Mark called Joan and threatened her. He said if she did not agree to a speedy settlement, so he could get some cash out of their present home, he would go to the adoption agency and tell them that they had committed fraud in signing for David when they weren't living together. This meant, of course, that David would be taken from Joan.

Joan called me that night in hysteria. She was certain that Mark would do just what he had threatened. I was concerned about her stability at this time. I tried to calm her down. If Mark succeeded in blackmailing her—which was exactly what he was trying to do—he would never stop. I also advised her—and this was the worst possible advice I could have given—that it might be in the best interests of the boy if she took him back to the agency so that he would be placed in a home where there were no threats of this nature.

Bless my sister, Leone. She was with Joan all through this terrible period in her life. The next day she called me. Joan had not slept all night; in fact, she had cried bitterly, thinking she might lose the boy. Leone wasted no time in telling me that my advice was poor, that if Joan lost David she would never make it through this ordeal. It was, of course, their decision, and I told her that if they wanted to keep the child, then we would have to call Mark's bluff.

The next day I called Sylvi's number and asked for Mark. He was there, of course, and I let him know where we stood. "Threats of blackmail will not solve this divorce or settlement any faster, nor will it get you your money any quicker. But if you want to play that way, Mark, it will drag things out and cost you both more money. The only one who will benefit will be the lawyers. If the whole estate is wasted, it will be your fault, no one else's. Don't forget," I added, "if the estate is gone, Joan and the boy will be taken care of. Our family will see to that."

Prior to this, sometime in mid-January, Joan realized it was past time to have David blessed in church. She wanted me to come down to Los Angeles and perform the ceremony, but Bishop Price told her that if Mark wanted to perform this function, it was his right to do so, regardless of his worthiness. She wanted me to call Bishop Price and discuss this. I did, and without my asking, he volunteered to me that Mark had admitted committing adultery. He did not mention names, but later we learned that Mark had been living with Sylvi Ingebrigtsen as early as December 30th, by his own admission. He had signed a police report on that date listing her address as his own.

After my conversation with Bishop Price, I was confused. From what he had told me, I could not understand why he hesitated to take action, in an ecclesiastical sense, against Mark. Early on the morning of February 1, I caught a flight to L.A. where Joan met me at the airport. We drove out to her home and I played with David until time for church. Leone, Joan and David, and I went to the church, then Joan and I left David in Leone's charge while she and I went into the bishop's office.

There were about twelve or fifteen people in his office but when the bishop saw Joan, he waved some papers over his head and said in a loud voice, "Joan, here are those marriage cancellation papers you requested." Joan was extremely embarrassed, and so was I. I had never seen a bishop perform an act so cruel and thoughtless in public. He was tactless.

On February 1st I blessed David. The bishop who had so carefully passed judgment on my worthiness to bless the boy, kept looking about to see if Mark would show up at the last minute. He didn't, of course.

Mark called Joan's lawyer on February 11th and said that he wanted a quick financial settlement, that he was willing to make some concessions if he could get it. He asked her lawyer to set up a meeting. During this time Mark told Joan openly that he was dating three girls. One of them happened to work at Sunn Classics and he had taken her to business lunches the previous fall while they were still married. Joan realized that this must have been Sylvi. Furthermore, Mark told her at this time that he couldn't tie up his money—he had to think of his future family. Here Joan quoted Mark's exact words adding, "David and I could have the house if I would give him $30,000."

In April Mark began bringing women to Joan's house, and in May Joan recorded:

> Mark finally came out to the house for a talk with me. He wanted me to know that any women he had ever been involved with was always on a subconscious level and that he never consciously sought anyone else. He knew he had to repent and needed my forgiveness—said that he had never lied to me about other women because I had never asked him.

Joan's notes continued:

> Mark had brought Sylvi...home to Idaho twice—once for a few hours on May 9th, Mother's Day, when he told them Sylvi was a secretary, and then June 20th for his brother's wedding. Mark then tried to take her home to his mother's to stay that evening but she refused to put them up. This time Mark told his family that Sylvi was an executive at Sunn Classics and second in command. Alyne (a sister) said Mark was crazy, and even their father told the family that Mark lies. On June 29th Mark made some very strong comments about the ERA law for women and said it was high time that women were brought down to his level.

In July, because of constant questions by the insurance company, Joan secured a copy of the police report of Mark's Porsche being stolen. The address and phone number on the report, filled out by Mark in December, were Sylvi's.

Joan was having other problems, too. Mark's support checks did not arrive regularly, and when they did, they often bounced. On June 30th, Joan received a notice of foreclosure on the house. Mark had not made payments as he had agreed to under court order.

On August 13th, Mark came to Joan with divorce papers. Joan's notes record:

> Mark came out to the house, profaned a lot, and finally struck me—became so irate he kicked in the front door. He then went to Bishop Price's and admitted to adultry

since our legal separation. I signed the divorce papers as he and Sylvi want to get married in 10 days or so.

Later that month Mark gave a deposition in San Diego where he perjured himself no less than seven times. He testified that he left Joan prior to the time they signed the final adoption papers for David, on December 19th. He said they separated on December 4th, 5th, or 6th, and further testified that he deliberately deceived the adoption agency until the papers were signed.

In another deposition, dated the following June, Mark admitted that he was living with another woman before signing the final adoption papers. He also signed the police report, admitting that he was living at Sylvi's address.

In San Diego on August 21st, Mark swore under oath that he had made no loans to Miss Sylvi Ingebrigtsen, the woman he was living with, nor that he had any interest in any property in joint ownership with Sylvi. Later in the same deposition he said that he loaned two thousand dollars to Sylvi and when he was asked where he got the money, he said from Goldstein Samuelson who were bankrupt. Later in the statement he added that he got it from the firm's receivers and that they paid him in cash. It takes a pathological liar to try to make people believe that a Federal Bankruptcy referee would pay money out in cash!

About two years later, Mrs. Norma Ann Waldren, a neighbor, testified under oath, on June 28, 1979, that she had been close friends of Mark's and Sylvi's since March or April, three years before. She met them, she said, because they were building homes next to each other, and Mark and Sylvi often came to see how their house was progressing under construction. Yet Mark had testified over five months after he had purchased this home, that there were no other holdings or community property! More perjury.

Because of Mark's attempt to blackmail Joan with the adoption agency, Joan's lawyers at this time asked Mark explicitly if he remembered signing the adoption papers where he agreed to the rights of inheritance for the child. He said yes.

Because of the biofrication the divorce was granted on August 23rd, 1976, and Mark married Sylvi in Salt Lake City on September 4th, at which time Shauna's husband maliciously called Joan long distance to ask if she knew where Mark was!

Joan received notice of default on the house on October 25th, in spite of the fact that Mark had been ordered to make house payments by the court! But worse was yet to come.

On December 6th (a sort of anniversary—almost a year to the day when Mark abandoned her and David) Mark came to see David and attempted to put his arms around Joan. He wanted even more than that, but Joan wasn't having any. She chewed him out and he responded by saying he merely wanted to comfort her.

This was not to be his last attempt at forcing himself on Joan. Joan's notes reveal that Mark seemed far more interested in her than in David. She received numerous calls from Mark, not to discuss David but to review his past actions. He said on one occasion, "I didn't lie to you, I just didn't answer when you asked me if I was going out with other women. I never consciously wanted to go out with other women."

Joan was fed up. Four months after he married Sylvi, Joan told him she didn't want to discuss his past or her future with him. He could make arrangements for visitation with David through their mutual friend, MarJean Lewis. It was around this time that Joan started getting strange phone calls, sometimes in the middle of the night. No one would talk. She heard only heavy breathing. When she accused Mark of this, he did not answer. This was his usual way of coping with guilt. Finally Joan changed to an unlisted number.

The time was fast approaching when Joan would have to give Mark $20,000 as his share of the community property settlement. In order to get the money she listed the house for sale, and because of Mark's harassment, she had come to the conclusion she would look for a house somewhere besides Southern California, to avoid living under those circumstances. This was a definite disadvantage. Nowhere else would she find a home base where she could be home every night and spend only seven days a month flying. But the situation there was unbearable.

In exchange for the $20,000 Mark was required by the court to give Joan copies of certain documents like income tax records, household insurance, etc., so that she would have no problems on her taxes, but during this time Joan continued to receive notices from the Internal Revenue Service. These she sent to her attorney who relayed them on to Mark or to his attorney. On one of Joan's visits to Salt Lake City she and I went over to the IRS and took a copy of the divorce decree. Regardless of the decree, or its provisions, they would collect the money from any party they could! If they could not get it from Mr. Wheeler, they would collect it from Joan, in spite of the court decree where he accepted liability.

This had been a major concern to Joan because Mark had always made out their income tax, with Joan merely signing it. He had not always declared all of his income. (He did not report the money he took from MarJean Lewis, for instance, or from Joan's mother or Jim Coleman. He had pocketed some of it but had not reported it as income.)

At the suggestion of the director of the IRS in Salt Lake, Joan sent the following letter to the IRS in Fresno, California. However, it did not stop the harassment.

December 10, 1977

INTERNAL REVENUE SERVICE
P.O. Box 11946
Fresno, California 93776

Miss Shirley Sherwood:

For nearly two years now, your office has been sending to me letters of notice of a tax deficiency. During this time, my former husband and I were in the process of getting a divorce. I received many notices from your office which I gave to my attorney. He gave them to Mr. Wheeler direct or on some occasions to Mr. Wheeler's attorney, Mr. Clark. He apparently has chosen to ignore all these letters. The divorce is final now and I am enclosing a portion of the court order where you will notice Mr. Wheeler agreed to hold me harmless in the event of any back owing taxes.

I hope this explanation will be satisfactory to you and helpful in getting this claim settled. I would like to request that any further correspondence be sent directly to Mr. Wheeler. His new address is:

> Mr. Mark Wheeler
> 19118 Vista Grande
> Northridge, California

If I can be of any help or cooperate with your office in disposing of this matter, I would be happy to do so.

> Cordially,
>
> Joan N. Wheeler

Nothing seemed to work out right for Joan. It was a period of total harassment, but perhaps things would be better for her when she moved. I sincerely hoped so. I didn't know how much the girl could stand. She had been buffeted by tides from all directions.

Sylvi—(Sunn) Classic Mother Figure

Mark's visits with David had always been sporatic. He called to make arrangements to pick the child up, but often he didn't show or he came hours later than he said he would. When David went with Mark, he always came home dirty and hungry, often without having had his diapers changed for the whole time.

Joan sold the house by the end of January, and by February 11th she applied for permission of the courts to move to Utah. Mark concurred with the idea. He wanted her to sell the house so he could get his money!

I took her out several times to look at homes, and one time I suggested that she consider a condominium or something smaller so that she wouldn't be strapped financially. She looked at me with something of surprise in her eyes. "Uncle Stan, I want a nice home in a good neighborhood so that David will have the stability of family and friends. I don't care how much of my income it takes to give him that."

Here she ran into problems, too. Real estate brokers

backed off from doing business with her. They said they couldn't get a mortgage for a single or a divorced woman. This happened so many times I decided it was ridiculous discrimination.

About this time Joan had to return to L.A. to fly, and she heard a rumor that Sunn Classics was contemplating moving their headquarters to Salt Lake City. This would upset all of her plans. Mark would be in Utah to harass her again. Since the court had given her permission to move to any location, she went to Colorado and began to look for a house there. In the meantime, she arranged for the movers to start packing. I flew to L.A. to help her get some of her heavy things ready.

Along with everything else Joan was concerned about, Saturday was Mark's normal visitation day, and David had been sick. The doctor prescribed medication four times daily and Joan felt she should telephone Mark about the medicine, for it was important David get it right on schedule.

She got Sylvi on the phone. When she started to tell the woman about David's medicine, Sylvi cut her off with a crude response. "Look, I would be a lot happier if you and that damned kid had never come into my life."

Joan was so startled, she was speechless. Quietly, she said, "Just tell Mark I called, and please tell him what I told you," and she hung up. I was on the extension phone. I hardly knew what to say. This was Mark's new wife, David's stepmother.

I wouldn't have been so startled if I had known what I know now. Sometime later a few things came out about Miss Sylvi Ingebrigtsen. She had been fired from her job at Sunn Classics, where she had been secretary to the President—and perhaps something more than that, according to rumor.

It wasn't the first time she had been fired.

In a deposition she testified that she had worked for American National Enterprises, Inc., in Salt Lake City in 1972, as secretary for Mr. Victor White, who managed the company. In February of 1973, Mr. Rip Colson replaced Mr. White and hired his own secretary. Sylvi became a file clerk and did general office work. In June of that year Mr. Raylan Jensen started as a salesman and traveled extensively for American National. Sylvi did his secretarial work and according to her own testimony, a "social and personal relationship developed" between the two of them. On June 10, 1974, Mr. Jensen left American National to work for Sunn Classics Pictures. One week later Sylvi left to go to work as his secretary at Sunn Classics. He was transferred to L.A. and almost immediately, Sylvi followed him. In her own words, "We traveled together, both for business and social reasons."

This was the same woman Mark told Joan stories about when he first started to work for Sunn Classics.

Her reign came to an abrupt halt, however, when the Chairman of the Board, Patrick Frawley, and not Mr. Jensen, came in and fired her. Why? When asked the last time she had seen Mr. Jensen, Sylvi confirmed that it was February or March of 1977, six months after she and Mark were married!

Mark made no attempt to see David on his birthday, but he did ask MarJean Lewis for his check of $20,000. Joan expressed willingness to give it to him if he would give her the documents the court ordered. He said he would get them together.

On Sunday, March 13th, Mark attempted to get the check from MarJean without giving her the papers. When she refused, we later learned Mark drove up to San Diego and drew up papers requesting a change in visitation rights, trying to use David as a lever against Joan to get her to turn this check over to him without the exchange of documents. He claimed that he had been kept from seeing his son by Joan and Louise and me for several months after Joan left California. Yet the paper was dated March 13th, and Joan didn't leave the state until March 14th.

Later that night Mark's lawyer called MarJean and attempted to intimidate her. Because of his statements, MarJean mailed the check to Mark.

When she learned what happened, Joan stayed overnight in Los Angeles to call the lawyer. She confirmed that she would give Mark the check immediately upon his compliance with the court order respecting the items Mark was to have turned over to her. After this conversation she went down to the bank and stopped payment on the check. The same day she wrote to the attorney as follows:

March 15, 1977

Mr. Robert C. Wood
1205 Prospect, Suite 400A
P.O. Box 1011
La Jolla, California 92038

Dear Mr. Wood,

This letter is to confirm our telephone conversation of Tuesday morning, March 15, 1977.

1. I told you that I had stopped payment on the check to Mr. Wheeler due to his refusal to turn over to me certain papers that he was ordered by the Court to provide me with. That no further payment would be made until Mr. Wheeler shows his respect by compliance with the Court order.

2. I was very disappointed that your office (Mr. Clark) would call up my friend, Mrs. Lewis, on Sunday, March 13th, 1977 at 10:45 P.M. and intimidate her by scare tactics. Mrs. Lewis was only trying to help me get Mr. Wheeler's money to him as soon as possible in exchange for the papers due me.

At which time you and Mr. Wheeler decide that you would like to comply with the Court order, just send the papers to the Salt Lake address that Mrs. Lewis provided you with. I will be happy to promptly send a check to any address Mr. Wheeler would like me to.

                Cordially,

                Joan N. Wheeler

Joan then left for Utah, but learning that Sunn Classics had indeed moved to Salt Lake City, she finally purchased a home in Englewood, Colorado. In the meantime she lived with both her sister Gail and Louise and me at our home. Several institutions had turned her down for a loan because she was single, in spite of the fact that her income was far in excess of the amount necessary to qualify. Finally after threat of a law suit, Western Savings and Loan in Denver gave Joan a loan for her house. When she went to sign the deed of trust and other papers, they were all made out to "Joan Newton Wheeler, an unmarried individual."

Several times during the week of March 21st, a process server tried to serve papers on Joan at my residence. Joan was not there at the time, so he was unable to serve them. She left for Denver shortly after, and again papers were delivered to my address for her.

On March 28th, Mark called and gave me his usual story. I was the only one in the family he could talk to. He desperately needed his $20,000 and wanted to know if I would help him. I told him that he could help himself. All he had to do was to comply with the court order and turn the papers over to Joan. He promised that if I would get his check, he would get the papers together, get on a plane and bring them right up to my office.

I said I would talk to Joan. She was out of town and was extremely upset with the way he had handled things. She might not be too disposed to be cooperative, and I could readily understand that.

He said that the papers to be served on Joan were for a change in visitation rights, that he was only trying to force

Joan into giving him his money. "Stan, if you will help me get the money, I will cancel those papers and not harass Joan any more. I would have no reason to. I don't have any interest in visitation rights to David if I can get my money." There was a short pause on the line, then he went on. "I'm going to have my own child, my own flesh and blood."

I told him I would get in touch with Joan and he could call me back in a week. He said he couldn't wait a week, that he was desperate.—Couldn't he call the next day? I told him he could.

I couldn't get hold of Joan for several days as she was flying. After finally discussing it with her, I advised her to give him the check and get rid of the situation since she had been successful in selling the house for more money than its appraisal. She said she would write the check out and send it to me, but I was not to give it to Mark until he turned over the four items she had been awarded.

I told Mark all of this when he called me on Friday. On Monday morning, bright and early, he walked into my office. He expressed deep appreciation for my help and assured me, without any prompting, that he had no interest in Joan or David because his wife was pregnant and they were going to have a child of their own. "After all," he said, "this is what every man wants, his own flesh and blood."

I checked through the papers and found that one of them was missing. I told him that I could not give the check to him until I got the other paper. He became quite upset but assured me that he would go back to L.A. that night and the missing paper would be delivered to my office by three o'clock the next day by special messenger of Sunn Classic would I give the check to the messenger at that time? I agreed to do so; however, I thought he should know that the check was not for the full $20,000. It was made out for $19,400.15. He wanted to know why. I told him that Joan had deducted two months' child support which the court had ordered him to pay and for which he was in arrears, plus some other charges which the court had ordered him to pay. I listed what they were and told him I thought this was only right. He acknowledged that they were due to Joan. This was the last money he would give to support David.

In actuality I had been quite sharp with Joan over the telephone. I thought she was being petty over $600, and taking a risk that he would open up the whole settlement again, but at approximately 2:30 the next afternoon a young lady from Sunn Classics office came in with an envelope addressed to me. She said she understood she was to get something in return. I opened the envelope and found what I needed, and then I handed her the check for Mark.

A few weeks later Mark called me again. He had found out that Joan had sold the house for more than he thought, and he was entitled to more money. For the first time I showed a lack of patience. "Mark, you forced the sale of that house because you needed the money so badly. Joan took the risk of selling the home. She might not have sold it, or she might have come up short and had to borrow to get you your $20,000. You were the one who forced this settlement. There is no reason why you should not abide by this agreement at this point!"

I went on. I was just getting warmed up. "I would think you would be embarrassed. Here was a young woman who worked and brought in good money for years while you were in the Navy. She sent you to school, paid thousands of dollars to have your teeth straightened, and bought this house with her own money, as well as many other things, all while you were getting on your feet. You always made far less than Joan, in fact, about half of her salary, and now, like a gigolo, you are trying to get everything you can from her! I will not help you get another red cent!"

When I informed Joan of the conversation, she had Mark use her brother Charley, who lived in Colorado Springs, as a new contact, as she had moved by then and was settled in that state. I was just as well satisfied. In all the times I had spoken to him, Mark had never once inquired about David, asked to see him or showed any interest in him except to get money. Frankly, I was disgusted. I didn't care if I never heard from Mark Wheeler again.

And as for his wife Sylvi, with her skimpy maternal instincts, I hoped that "damned kid" would never have to rely upon her as a mother figure. What did Sylvi have to take Mark away from Joan? I pictured the woman as a sort of Anita Ekberg, skilled in the arts of the modern-day courtesan. Imagine my surprise when I first saw her at the custody hearing. My blonde Swedish bombshell could only be described as "prematurely matronly."

A Rock In Time Of Trouble

Leone Mann Hartley Newton, Joan's mother, was a steady support to her daughter during her many months of trial with Mark. But then, she was that kind of woman! More like a mother to me than a sister, I remember Leone as a rock of Gibraltar, a willing confidante, and a mother substitute who spoiled me, I'm afraid. We were very close.

Leone was the one who slipped me five dollars and loaned me her car when I had a special date. She even told me about the birds and the bees when I was younger, and I recall that she and I, along with other members of the family, spent long, hard hours throwing hay, cutting asparagus, and bunching radishes side by side all through my growing years.

Leone was a hard worker. Besides laboring in the fields, she worked at O. J. Kirk's as a clerk during the depression and bought her father, who was the sheriff, a suit so that he could attend to his church duties as a high councilman properly dressed. She ran against her husband later on in an election for Justice of the Peace, and won, and she was called upon to sentence her own friends and neighbors in that position. But she handled the sticky assignment well. Never one to bad-talk, Leone was well-liked and respected. When she dressed up, she could pass as a member of the Women's League, and yet nothing was beneath her dignity when it came to helping anyone out.

For years she hand-dipped chocolates as a means of income during tight times, but even after finances no longer dictated this as a means of livelihood, friends and acquaintances called on Leone to furnish them with her famous hand-dipped holiday treats.

Leone was a rarity, a gentle, hard working lady. And in spite of the troubled home Joan grew up in, she and her mother became closer as the years wore on. Leone had bequeathed her ability to work to Joan, and Joan recognized the part her mother had played in her early life perhaps earlier than most young people. Besides, Joan was always properly respectful toward her parents, her mother who deserved that respect, as well as her father, who sometimes did not.

Leone was a delicate child. She suffered from a heart problem and several bouts with pneumonia during the first few years of her life, and there must have been times when Grandma Mann wondered if she would raise her second born. But she did, although Leone herself used to tell a story about old Doctor Kesler, who delivered all of her mother's children except me. Whenever Leone and her mother would run into Doctor Kesler on the streets of Bountiful, he would stop her and say, "Well, Nellie, this is a child you robbed from the grave!"

Despite her precarious beginning, Leone enjoyed vigorous health right up to the time of the exploratory tests which took her life. She was an active woman. Besides rearing four children of her own, she was busy with church and civic affairs. She served as Justice of the Peace for many years and worked at Farmers' State Bank for over twenty years. In her retirement years she traveled extensively, through Europe with Louise and me, in the orient with Joan, again through Europe with her sister, and over all of the United States at various times. She was a woman who enjoyed living. When she went to Europe with us, we were hard pressed to keep up with her. She was willing to try anything and she wanted to see it all!

Not one to show favoritism, she loved all of her children, but it must have hurt her deeply to see her youngest daughter treated so shabbily by her husband. Joan was always such a loving child, and her mother knew she deserved better. She helped as much as she could through all of Joan's problems.

Some of the time she lived with Joan in California, partly to care for David while Joan flew, but also to give her the moral support she needed. And when she wasn't actually with her, she tried to comfort Joan through letters. Joan's file included some notes from her mother that she must have treasured.

Excerpts from a note dated July 31, 1977, read:

Dear Joan—

I'm not too surprised at the outcome of the (church) court. After this long I felt sure it would be in Mark's favor.... In spite of how things look now, I still feel maybe the sequence of events are happening for the best. This I do know, that the Lord loves you and is watching over you....

Keep smiling. Things are always blackest before the dawn. I love you very much and think and pray for you and David each day.

       Mother

Another note, undated, said:

Dear Joan—

Couldn't sleep after I talked to you last night. I feel so

inadequate and helpless to do or say something that will help lighten your problem.

You said that no one was dependent on you, and no one needed you—and that just isn't right. I *need* you and love you very much. You and I have had a closer relationship and communicated better than I have with my other children. Gail has been very precious and dear, but she is rather withdrawn and it was hard to get close to her. Charley has been close during his problems but the feeling leaves there. Shauna has always held me at arm's length, but with you I have been closer and have been able to let my hair down more. You have seen my weaknesses more than my other children.

Don't ever feel that no one cares—it just isn't so. The Lord cares deeply and is there to give comfort and help—if you will only ask Him—then *listen*. Don't become impatient for an answer. Just keep waiting and doing all you can to bring about the solution you are hoping and praying for. "We ask the Lord for strength and he gives us problems." Solving these problems makes us strong.

Keep your chin up, darling. I love you very much.

Mother

And she wrote just before she went into the hospital, on August 8, 1977:

Dear Joan and David—

I want you to know how much I love you two. I have felt terrible since I talked to you last Friday. Praying that the Lord will bless you and help you to soften your feelings about what has happened recently. Bishop Peterson told you that the Lord works in mysterious ways to bring about many things. So please try to think *Positive*. Try to forget the past and live and work for the future. I know there is a good one for you....

Keep your chin up, darling. All my love,

>Mother

Leone stood by Joan when she moved to Denver. She had no end of trouble. Her new house had flaws which the builder saw fit to ignore, and the men who put in her lawn did a shoddy job—and expected her to pay them double if they replaced the sod. She also had car troubles, the most aggravating of all. She sold her last car after only nine months because of some minor electrical problem which no one seemed to be able to repair. After taking a three-thousand-dollar loss and buying another car, she found that the new one didn't start half of the time! On top of that, a drunk rammed into her one night and when the insurance company learned that he had no insurance, Joan had to pay the deductible to get her car fixed, even though the other driver was cited. Through all these annoyances, Leone was there to lend a helping hand. Joan had no one else. As a single woman she was on her own, both financially and emotionally.

Leone was such a comfort to Joan that she grew to rely on her mother's encouragement. It became a family joke. Whenever Leone would complain of a tiny ache or a head cold, Joan would pull a face and cry, "Don't you dare die and leave me alone in this mess!"

But Leone did die. And she left Joan in a mess. What was supposed to be a routine medical procedure turned into a fatal experience and Leone died in the hospital. In addition to all of her other problems, now Joan had to face the loss of her mother, her best friend on earth.

Shauna, the Family Adversary

After Leone's death, when Joan went over to Shauna's before the girls were to meet to select burial clothing for their mother, Joan asked Shauna if they couldn't forget past problems and become friends. "I'd like to call you for lunch, Shauna, and bring David to visit."

Shauna answered, "What for? Let's just say we parted. I'm not interested."

Not even at the time of her mother's death could Shauna bring herself to overlook years of accumulated hatreds. This shouldn't have surprised us. I recalled a number of dramatic episodes.

About the middle of June, in 1975, I spent some time in Salt Lake City making contacts and investigating the possibility of buying a company so we could return to Salt Lake City to live, and Leone came to visit us at our condominium at Park City. She approached me about her will and trust, which Dave Young, Shauna's husband, had drawn up for her with him as the trustee and executor on his recommendation. Some of her other children were unhappy about this; in fact, she was unhappy, too. She showed me a letter Dave had written to her on March 13, 1975. It was not only impersonal, it was rude!

I was going to be back in Salt Lake City in two weeks and I told her I would go over her will at that time. In closing I asked her what, specifically, she was upset about. She mentioned she didn't even have a copy of the will, and when she asked for one, Dave always had an excuse. "Yes," he would say, "I'll have one of the girls make you a copy. I'll send it to you." But it never came.

And Shauna had made some comments in Leone's hearing about the will, and they didn't tally with the way Leone wanted it drawn up.

Two weeks later Leone came up to Park City to visit and we had a chance to talk. She wanted us to get a copy of her will so that she could have it changed. She had also asked Dave several times to return her safety deposit key which she entrusted to him, but he always had an excuse not to do so. She insisted that I go with her to the bank that day so that she could change her box and have me sign with her.

Once started, it was hard for her to stop. She enumerated things that she had witnessed. First, she said that Shauna had taken practically everything out of her father's house, including items he had promised to Joan and others. When Leone talked to Shauna about this, the girl said she had a bill of sale for each of the items. People at the grocery store where C.W. bought his supplies said Shauna had been coming in with him weekly for quite a few months, buying about $20.00 worth of groceries, writing a check for $100.00 on C.W.'s account, and pocketing the cash! Leone also found out that Shauna had been writing checks on his account for her children's piano and dancing lessons.

Leone went on. The children had bought C.W. a color TV the Christmas prior to that year, but he was unhappy with it. Leone offered to buy the set. She gave Shauna a check for $500.00 in payment, which Shauna was supposed to deposit in her father's account. Later Leone learned that the check went into Shauna's account. It never found its way into C.W.'s hand.

Shauna and Dave did not restrict their activities to family. They purchased a home which belonged to Rhoda Johnson, heir to substantial holdings of several corporations founded by the Hogle family in Salt Lake, and Dave had been appointed executor for Mrs. Johnson, who was elderly and living in a rest home. Leone related a number of improprieties she had become aware of regarding Dave's handling of Mrs. Johnson's estate. These improprieties were cause of great concern to her and for this reason she wanted to remove Dave from handling any part of her own estate.

Until this time, Shauna had been handling her father's finances. She purchased treasury notes in excess of $8,000 for her father at the time he sold his home, and they had placed them in his safety deposit box. The very next day, for some reason, C.W. felt insecure about them and he asked another member of his family to drive him down to the bank. Not one certificate was in the box! Shauna had signed in that very day, before her father's arrival.

Now I was disturbed. I held Dave in high regard, and I thought Shauna had grown out of some of the frightening traits she displayed as a youngster. However, I knew my sister: she never lied. She didn't even have tendencies toward exaggeration.

There was no love lost between my sister and C.W. at this time. They had been divorced for a number of years, but still, Leone hated to see the old man duped out of his estate. Little did we know that just a few months prior to our talk, C.W. had written a codicil to his last will and testament wherein he set aside his appointment of his daughter Shauna as executrix of his will and named Zion's Bank and Trust.

On the same day that I signed on Leone's bank box, she called Dave and said she was coming to Salt Lake to pick up a copy of her will. If he wasn't going to be in his office, he should leave a copy for her. But when she arrived at Dave's office he was there. She had anticipated a visit of ten or fifteen minutes at the most, but he kept her for hours, trying to talk her out of changing the will and trust. She finally took her copy and left the office.

Later I read it. I was frankly appalled at the powers Dave had given himself. He held total discretionary judgment for purposes of having Leone declared incompetent, for evaluating items in her estate and for taking whatever items he wanted at the value he set before her property was disposed of. I asked her if this was what she had directed him to do. She said absolutely not. That same day she wrote Dave a note, telling him that she wanted to revoke the trust for the best interests of all the family.

I purchased a company shortly after this, and trying to keep things in the family, I engaged Dave to draw up the contracts. I ended up in no end of legal entanglements because of his incompetency both in drawing up the contract and in following through with my end of the purchase. I finally lost the purchase of that firm and had to find another one to buy. I ended up in litigation over the first deal. I determined never to have Dave handle any more legal work for me, so when a friend of mine in New Jersey recommended a lawyer with experience in this line, I set up an appointment with him. When I told Dave and informed him that I needed my files, he insisted on knowing who the attorney was. I told him, reluctantly, and assured him that the reason I was engaging him was that he had more experience in Utah with this kind of litigation. Dave hastily wrote a note "introducing" me to this new attorney as his client and had the note delivered without my knowledge.

During the next few months Dave called me on a number

of occasions pleading with me to talk Leone out of changing her will. I told him she needed peace of mind, and if changing her will would give it to her, then that was exactly what she should do. He asked repeatedly if I were the new trustee. I told him I wasn't. Then he wanted to know who was, but I informed him that this was confidential. If he wanted to know, he should ask Leone.

From this time forward our relationship started to cool; however, once he came and told me he desperately needed help. His wife was going to the library and searching the scriptures to find evidence justifying children turning against their parents. In fact she stated that she wanted her name taken off all family records in the archives. He said it was obviously an emotional thing with Shauna, and he was concerned about her mental health. (Sometime later Shauna's bishop intimated to us that Shauna was seriously ill. From the way he talked, those present immediately thought of cancer or some other fatal sickness. But the more we thought about it, the more it impressed us that she might be having severe emotional problems as Dave had suggested. The bishop went on. "She has been so worried about her father," he said with compassion. Shauna? Worried?—About her father? I couldn't believe that. Whatever her illness, it had not been brought on by worry about her father. Gail later confirmed that she knew nothing about any health problems Shauna might be having.)

Dave wanted to talk about the problems between Shauna and the rest of the family. I did not want to discuss anything with him unless Shauna were present, and of course, Shauna refused to meet with us. As far as I was concerned, the matter was dropped. But Dave pleaded with me to try to get Leone to make up with Shauna and to visit them when she returned to Utah. (Leone was living with Joan in California at this time.) I said I would try.

Some weeks later when Leone was staying with us, I

suggested we drive over to Shauna's. Leone was reluctant. She was tired of being snubbed and humiliated by her daughter. However, I prevailed on her to go over and visit. Shauna was gracious and friendly to my wife and me, but she snubbed her mother completely, never directed any conversation to her, and was extremely rude. When we left, Leone was in tears, and I apologized for having pushed her into that situation.

About this time Joan came to Salt Lake to see me at my office. She had just met with her father's attorney and found out all the things that Shauna had done to C.W. In particular, she learned about the suit C.W. filed against Shauna. The attorneys were concerned about taking it to court because time had elapsed since he initiated the suit and his condition had deteriorated. No wonder, he had been placed in a rest home as a charity patient!—Even though he had funds coming in monthly and should have had money in his savings account. Joan was unaware that the money had made its way out of C.W.'s savings account. It was not until they were settling her father's estate that she learned there was no reckoning of such money.

The day after Leone's funeral Joan went to see her father at the rest home where she discovered he was a charity patient. Joan was aghast to learn from the staff that Shauna and Dave, whom she introduced as her "attorney," not her husband, had just been to see C.W. Shauna called the old man "Daddy" and made herself a general nuisance. Knowing about C.W.'s savings and his monthly income from the sale of his home, Joan confronted Shauna about C.W.'s charity status. Shauna alibied, "Oh, I took $8,000 and put it in another bank where the rest of the family couldn't get at it." Joan asked which bank, but her sister refused to tell her.

Prior to this incident, C.W. asked Shauna for the return of his funds. He insisted that Shauna had taken them without his knowledge or permission. When she refused, he took steps to file a suit against her. He even added a second codicil to his will, directing that if this money and the items removed from his home were not returned, Shauna would be cut out of his will. He wanted the household goods gathered and divided among his children. He did not know there was nothing left to divide. Everything had been confiscated. We later saw them in the Young's home.

While C.W. was still living with his older daughters, before he went to the rest home, Shauna had a meeting with his first family. They had called the meeting when they discovered that unusual expenditures had been drawn on C.W.'s account. Shauna was undaunted. She assured them that it would simply be one family against the other because Joan would back her. The lawyers wondered if they had a case if this were so. Joan knew nothing about this, of course, and would not have sided with Shauna against her father in any event. After this meeting, Zion's Bank was appointed trustee of C.W.'s estate—what remained of it.

I talked with Bennett Peterson, the Bountiful attorney who met with the group. He said that he had to order all of them out of his office because of their shouting and vulgar language. He expressed surprise at Shauna's participation in this kind of behavior. He had attended school with her and had never seen this side of her personality before. I couldn't explain her behavior. I simply repeated what Joan had instructed me: that she would cooperate with them in any manner to secure her father's financial position.

In early August of 1977, Leone came to Salt Lake City to have some tests taken at LDS Hospital. Louise took her over and signed her in and the tests were to be administered the next day. Leone had expressed fear of the procedure, but we thought that only natural—no one likes to have their body tampered with. We sent our daughter Micalle over to visit her after the tests, but as the girl walked into the room, the doctors were working frantically over Leone. She had suffered a stroke in the process of the test, and they had brought her back to her room. When Micalle called us at the office, we didn't know how serious it was. However, the next day, after seeing her and talking with the doctor, I knew her condition warranted notifying her children. I finally reached Charley and Joan in Colorado, and I was trying to reach Gail who was on her way to Florida. I decided purposely not to call Shauna on the basis of a statement that Leone made to me. "If I was sick and woke up and saw Shauna there, I would know I was dying." I was afraid that it would be too great a shock if she should wake and find Shauna at her side.

Leone never came out of her coma. She died on August 15, 1977, and her services were held at the Bountiful Mortuary at Shauna's insistence. Leone had been active in her church and should, rightfully, have had services at the West Bountiful Ward.

After the funeral, Charley Mann, my brother, asked each of the children to meet him at Gail's the following day to discuss the will. As soon as we returned home, Dave Young called me. He said he didn't know how to approach this, but he didn't want Shauna embarrassed. If she had been cut out of her mother's will, she would rather not go to Gail's and find out in front of everyone. Could I inform him about the situation? I told Dave that neither he nor his wife knew Leone very well or they wouldn't have thought such a thing. She was not a bitter or vindictive person, no matter how she had been treated. I knew for a fact that Shauna had not been cut out of her mother's will.

The next day you would have thought Shauna had showered her mother with presents. She wanted everything in sight. When some pearl earrings were brought out, Joan quietly mentioned that she had bought them for Leone in Hong Kong and they were real pearls. Despite Joan's statement, Shauna claimed them and she and Dave chewed on them to determine if they were, indeed, real. It was hard to believe someone could be so greedy, especially when, the day before, they thought they had been left out of the will!

When we were going through Leone's pictures and genealogical records, something upset Shauna and she finally stomped out of my home calling all of the Manns "damned asses." (Later she denied her words. "I did not call you damned asses!" she declared. "I called you 'ass holes!'" —A decided improvement.)

Nevertheless, several days later I attempted to solve all of the family problems because Leone's memory was fresh in my mind and I felt this might be the last thing I could do for my sister. I called Dave and asked if my brother Charley and I could come up and talk to him. He agreed.

The conversation that took place that night would fill a book. Shauna and Dave absolutely refused to return the things they had taken from C.W.'s estate. They said possession was nine-tenths of the law. I asked them about the things C.W. had given Joan as a wedding present. The old man had written out a list of the things he wanted her to have on a nice wedding card which he had notorized at the Farmers' State Bank in Woods Cross. Shauna and Dave didn't bother to deny that they had taken them out of C.W.'s home. But Dave claimed he had a bill of sale for them, as well as for all the other items they had removed.

Looking him straight in the eye, I asked Dave if he knew something was ethically and morally wrong, but he could accomplish it through a legal technicality and the decision was entirely his, would he do it? He thought it through before he answered, but finally he said, "Yes, I would."

During the period of time that the bills of sales were signed, Joan and her mother had taken C.W. to an opthalmalogist in Bountiful. In sorting out Leone's things, we found an old envelope with a notation in her handwriting concerning the doctor's diagnosis: "no cataracts, lost most of his vision, retina deteriorated, can't give any help. Legally blind."

There was no possibility C.W. could have read anything he signed, at that time or later.

While we were sorting out other papers, we also came upon a bill of sale made out to Shauna and Dave for a concert grand piano. The sale price?—*One dollar.*

C.W.—Victim of His Own Child's Greed

When Shauna cleaned out all of the things from her father's home, she also took records and pictures that pertained to Mr. Newton's first family. She couldn't have had any interest in them—she was his second wife's child—and it is difficult to see why she latched on to them. She certainly didn't have any right to them, but they never found their way back to the children by the first wife, and no one knows what happened to them.

Joan was from a different mold. She had saved a lot of time for Christmas, 1977, and when she came to our house for the usual holiday celebration a few days before Christmas, she didn't leave until January 9th. It was a fun season. David was at the age when he kept everyone busy. I made the mistake of pushing him on a bicycle and then running to catch up with him, and he had me running during the whole vacation. I loved it.

Joan spent a lot of time shopping and preparing for the holidays and in addition she went over to the rest home to visit with her aged father, C.W., about every other day. Often she'd clean her father up, take him out for a ride, and sometimes bring him to our home for lunch. I admired the girl for the way she treated her father, especially in view of the kind of father he had been to her. She loved and respected him, and she manifested those feelings in her actions. At the end of her leave, we took her to the airport and we had hardly been home an hour when a lady from the rest home called. Joan had given them our phone number in case of emergency. Early that morning C.W. had started to fade rapidly. The doctor said he would probably not last more than an hour.

They had attempted to call his children, initially his first wife's family, but they were unable to reach any of them. Then they called Shauna who told them she had a dentist's appointment and in spite of the fact that her father was dying, Shauna said that she could not come.

Thirty minutes later he had passed away and they were at a loss as to where they should send the body. This was when they called us. We informed them that we had just put Joan on a plane to Los Angeles, but that the plane would be landing about that time, and we would have her paged.

Within three hours Joan was back in Salt Lake City, but before she even arrived, she called and told us where to take her father's remains. In the meantime at the direction of a son of C.W.'s first wife, another mortuary had taken over. At least arrangements were made.

On January 11th, C.W.'s first family told Joan and me that Shauna had been down to the Bricklayer's Union within three hours after his death to file for payment of the insurance money. Yet she had been too busy to go to his side when he was dying! True, she was the beneficiary, but the will stipulated that the funds were to be used to pay off C.W.'s debts at the time of his burial. Shauna did not pay the debts, nor did the money ever find its way into the estate.

About three o'clock that afternoon Joan came by my office.

I could tell that she was extremely upset. She proceeded to discuss everything we had been through when I first returned to Utah. At the time the lawyer had given her a copy of C.W.'s last will and testament, signed in January, 1973, in which his daughter Shauna was named as executrix, and also a copy of the first codicil to his last will and testament, dated February 12, 1975, wherein he removed Shauna as executrix and appointed Zion's First National Bank of Salt Lake City. He also handed her a copy of the trust agreement he had signed on May 14, 1975, which was prepared by Bennett Peterson, Bountiful attorney, and named Zion's First National Bank as trustee of his trust. Another paper which she received at this time was a second codicil to his last will and testament, dated August 2, 1975. The second paragraph reads as follows:

> In my last Will I therein provided that my said daughter, Shauna N. Young, should share equally with my four other children, but having recently discovered that my daughter, Shauna, has removed from my bank accounts funds of considerable amounts without my consent; and I state that Shauna has been asked to return to me said amounts, but that she has not refunded any sum whatsoever, so I now revoke that part of my will wherein I bequeathed to Shauna a one-fifth part of my estate, and in lieu thereof, I now provide that Shauna shall not receive that portion, or any portion, unless she returns to me or to my Trustee the sums so taken from my bank account, which amount I estimate to be and set at the sum of $10,000.00. If this sum is returned to me or to my Trustee, then she shall share equally with my other children.

Shortly after, on November 28, 1975, acting through his attorney, C.W. had filed a complaint in District Court, Davis County, State of Utah, Number 234178 and Civil Court Number 21241, detailing Shauna's theft of funds amounting to the sum of over $16,000.00 which she had taken and refused repeatedly to return.

Joan was in tears. She felt alone and deserted. None of the rest of her family had taken any stand or expressed any feelings about the way Shauna had treated their father. Although C.W. and I had never had words, she knew I had not admired the man but she asked me to represent her at the meetings called by Zion's Bank and Trust to try to straighten things out, and I agreed to help her.

She pulled out a blanket power of attorney which she had made out to me, officially. I explained that I was willing to carry out her directions but that it was not my place to make any decisions regarding the estate or action against Shauna. I didn't have to make any decisions. Joan knew what she wanted and she was explicit in her instructions:

"First, I want whatever money is left in the estate to be used to pay my father's debts, and then I want the rest home reimbursed for the money that was paid out for him as a charity patient, to clear his name, even if it takes every bit of money left. And I want to see that the suit my father started against Shauna is pursued and concluded."

I relayed this information to the Trust Officer at Zion's Bank and Trust, and in a matter of days the bank called Shauna and asked her to come in. She refused.

They called back several times. Finally Dave, her husband, went in to represent her. Apparently they informed him about the position Joan was taking regarding the legal action of her father, and they also gave Dave a copy of the letter which Joan had received from her father in which C.W. notarized the gift of several things he wanted Joan to have. Dave acknowledged that he and Shauna had them in their possession and that they might be willing to negotiate for some of the items.

During this conversation they learned that these instructions had been given through me by Joan. Shortly after, I received a phone call from Dave. I had previously kept quiet about these matters because I knew they would cause immediate problems. I was right. Now everything was out in the open. They knew that I was fully aware of the things they had done. Dave wasted no time in telling me to keep my nose out of it, that it was none of my business. He made the mistake of telling the bank the same thing, and they informed him, as I did, that I had a blanket power of attorney to represent Joan.

From this time on, Shauna and Dave were so bitter toward me they both went out of their way to fabricate lies about me and other members of the Mann family, even those who were not involved in the matter. In no way did I want to chose between one niece and another, especially when they were both children of my dead sister, Leone. We wanted to make everyone feel members of the family, but we were given no choice. The choice was made by Shauna and Dave. They felt such resentment towards Joan that they would try to subvert everything in her last will and testament as well as the wishes she had for her son.

There were several meetings with Zion's Bank and Trust. The three children from C.W.'s first wife, Joan, myself, bank personnel and Bennett Peterson were present when it was outlined what chances they had with the suit. C.W. had made the codicils out purposely to cut Shauna out of his will, but nothing had been done about the trust which was held by the bank. It had simply been ignored, even though Mr. Newton's desires were plain.

On April 26, 1978, Dave Young filed a motion to dismiss C.W. Newton's suit against Shauna on the basis of his death. The time allowed for anyone to act on the motion had only two days to run when Joan and I learned of the situation. At that time Joan told the bank that she wanted to take action on it, and I later confirmed this by telephone.

Nevertheless it was the bank's decision to let it expire

intentionally. Neither Zion's Bank nor Bennett Peterson had accomplished C.W.'s wishes nor had they acted on the wishes of the heirs of the estate and trust. In fact, when Judge Durham heard the case, she apologized openly in court for the decision she had to hand down. She said it was obvious what Mr. Newton's intentions were, that he did not want Shauna to share in anything that he had left, but that it had not been handled in the proper technical manner to accomplish his wishes. "This leaves me no alternative but to rule that Shauna will also share equally in what is in the trust."

All through this experience it was obvious that law and justice are two separate things, and that they are moving farther apart all the time. It would appear judges and lawyers are the biggest hindrance to justice and they share the burden equally. They are responsible for the morass the American public has slumped into. Only our courts have the power to correct injustices inflicted upon our citizens daily. Political abuses, graft, pay-offs, and white-collar crime could not exist in a justice-oriented society, but they flourish in a bureaucracy built by the legal profession. A legal technicality will prevail even though it prevents the obvious intent of the law.

C.W. Newton was just one victim of injustice. Unfortunately, he was victimized by his own daughter. And now that he is dead, he can do nothing about it.

The Source of It All

We were having lunch at our house on August 27th when Joan asked if she could speak to me privately. This wasn't too unusual, for she had sought my advice on a number of occasions since her divorce, but for some reason I knew this was special.

She came right to the point. "My mother always looked to you for help and counsel, Uncle Stan, and through the years I jumped at every chance to come to your place because it was so bad at home." Here she paused for a moment, thoughtfully, then she went on. "In many ways you have been more than an uncle to me. More like a father." It was true.

She continued. "I have no where else to turn. I need to ask several favors of you." First, she asked us to serve as surrogate grandparents for her son. We were delighted. That was no favor. I was hardly surprised, for the boy had seemed like a grandson to us, anyway, because of the relationship which had built up during their frequent visits.

The next favor floored me. She asked me to serve as

executor of her estate and trustee of the trust that she wanted to be set up for David. And she wondered if we would be willing to take the boy into our home and raise him, adopting him as our own, should anything happen to her.

I was not prepared for this, and I explained as much to Joan. Her sister Gail and her husband Glenn were as nice a couple as you'd ever find, and I thought they had a wonderful home. She could not find a better environment anywhere for David. I was certain Gail and Glenn would be happy to have the child if he ever needed a home.

She hesitated. "Uncle Stan, I feel the same way you do about Gail and Glenn and their home. But I've thought about this for some time—it isn't just a passing concern. In talking to them about my problems I've sensed that they do not really think the circumstances were as I related them." She was referring, of course, to the situations with Mark. "Their philosophy is that you should go to all lengths to insure peace and harmony between family members, and their outlook is very Pollyanna-ish. I couldn't rely on them to fight for David's rights if anything happened to me."

She was right. Gail and Glenn, good people, sure enough, often ignored the hard, cold facts of life.

Joan went on. "As sure as I am facing you here, if anything should happen to me, Mark would attempt to get whatever estate there was, even if it meant taking David, and you know, Uncle Stan, he has no interest in him. You and Aunt Louise are the only ones who have believed the things I was going through with Mark."

I had several reactions. One was guilt. On several occasions when Joan had related things to me about Mark, I felt she was imagining them, that she was biased in her observations, but because I loved her, I said nothing, only offered her the comfort and support she needed at the time. Then, too, I felt she was mistaken about Mark's interest in David's trust. After all, Mark himself had told me that he had no interest in David whatsoever. He clearly differentiated between David and the child his wife was expecting, his "own flesh and blood," as he put it. Surely he wouldn't have the gall to attempt to get control of any money that might develop as a result of Joan's demise.

Joan said, "Uncle Stan, you still don't comprehend the kind of an individual he is. Mark will go to any length to get material things." She pleaded with me. "You are the only one I can depend on. If you never do another thing for me, please do this."

What could I say? "If you feel this strongly about it, Joan, of course I will. Let me talk to Aunt Louise first. If I were to adopt David, he would be heir to my estate. That's entirely my decision, still, I want Louise and the kids reaction before I do anything." She said she understood, but could I please talk to them right away? She would like to have the matter settled before she left Salt Lake. She hesitated to get on another plane until something was written up to take care of David.

She showed me the wills she had drawn up in California to specifically preclude Mark from getting control of or influence over the money from her estate. She asked if I knew a Utah lawyer that we could engage right away to draw the necessary papers. I called my neighbor who was an attorney, but I could not reach him.

That afternoon I disclosed the subject of our talk to each of my children. I explained the situation and what Joan was asking us to do. They expressed complete agreement. They had spent a lot of time with David and they loved him like a brother. That night when David came to kiss us goodnight, he called us Grandma and Grandpa for the first time. "Mama told me you are going to be my grandma and grandpa, but she still has to call you Uncle Stan and Aunt Louise. Are you going to be my grandma and grandpa for ever and ever?" We assured him that this was so, and he gave us each a big hug and ran off to bed.

Shortly after this change in our relationship—was it really a change? We had always felt this way about him—we started the "love game." David would say, "You know, Grandma and Grandpa, I love you clear over to my place and back, over the ocean and to the mountains, and clear up to the sky and back."

He made a beeline for our bedroom when he came to visit. Immediately he would spot his picture and say, "That's me." On one occasion when he has just been corrected about something, he said he was going to run away. I asked him why. He said, "Well, when my friend in Colorado gets mad, he runs away." I told him it was no fun to run away alone, that he should always take a friend. "Do you want me to run away with you?" I asked. He answered, "Yes," so we went to the basement, got a sleeping bag and came upstairs for some books.

He helped me select the books and we went into the bedroom, laid out the sleeping bag and crawled into it together, talking about how much fun it was to run away. Little did I know that we had started a tradition. He and I ran away many times together and read books—but we had to crawl into the sleeping bag each time. Reading together on the bed was not running away!

After my abortive attempt to contact my neighbor who was a lawyer, my daughter suggested the name of another neighbor who was also an attorney. I hadn't even been aware of his profession, but I called him and he was good enough to come to the house that afternoon to see Joan. When he came, I started to leave the room, but Joan wanted me to hear everything.

At this first meeting with her attorney, Byron Fisher, Joan openly and clearly explained the bad relationship that had existed between her and her sister Shauna from the time they were little children up to the present. She reviewed briefly her own marital problems and then proceeded to tell him what she wanted done. To my amazement, she instructed him that she wanted all of her personal property left to Louise and me. At this point I stopped her.

"What about Charley and Gail?" I asked.

She dismissed my question, saying that there had never been any relationship with her brother. He never visited her or even inquired about her all the time she had lived in Colorado. Even her mother had noticed this, and Leone had talked with Charley about it. Joan went on. She had never received any support from Gail and Glenn, even though they had been "nice" to her. Then she repeated her experience with Shauna when she had tried to get together with her on some semblance of a relationship and had been met with indifference.

Out of fairness to the rest of the family, I suggested that her feelings would change about this as time went on, and I asked Byron if there were a way that this could be handled without the entire will being changed. He said yes, there was a way. They could insert a clause that stated she would leave a list of her personal things and their disposal. She should prepare such a list and sign it, making sure it was with her will or in her safety deposit box where it would be readily found.

He left us. In a few hours he returned with a handwritten document which he witnessed. He told Joan it would suffice until he could have the official documents drawn up and properly signed and executed. Joan was noticeably relieved.

She and David stayed a few days with us, then she returned to Denver where she was scheduled to fly. She was to be gone only two days, but as I took her to the airport, I felt impressed to put my arm around her. I told her that we loved her, that our home was her home and would always be. We stood there in the terminal, both of us crying as passers-by gawked. A sad farewell, they probably thought. Nothing could have been farther from the truth. We were happy. She had been able to provide for her son, and I was able to serve a member of my family.

In a few days she returned. But before she and David left for Denver, she told me she was aware that there was one adult grave left on the George B. Mann plot, next to her mother's grave. Since I was executor of that estate, could she have it? I told her I would see that it was hers.

The grief of her mother's passing had been overwhelming to Joan at first. Until this time Joan had been a brick, but when she returned to Denver, at least three times a week we found ourselves talking long distance, either at her instigation or ours, and we grew even closer. At times her role as a divorced woman tested her to the limit. She got static from landscapers, subcontractors, and even the builder of her home who didn't seem to want to comply with the contract he had made. Sometimes Joan's calls came late at night, and I did not understand her problems as I should have. I turned the phone over to Louise, who fortunately compensated when I failed.

During this period of difficulties, people in Joan's church in Colorado came to her aid. Shortly after her mother died, Bishop Peterson went out of his way to provide Joan with moral and spiritual uplift. It was greatly needed. Joan had attempted to put her bitterness about her divorce behind her, and at my suggestion, she had not aired her problems, but Bishop Peterson perceptively probed the matter to see if he could help.

She called to see what I thought she should do. All bishops were not like Bishop Price, I told her. She had been terribly disappointed and disillusioned about his callousness. Only after her mother passed away did he finally write Joan a letter apologizing for not keeping his word over a personal problem she had confided to him. We eventually obtained a copy of the letter he finally wrote and the information he relayed was false, even contrary to what he had discussed with me personally regarding his relationship with both Joan and Mark during their divorce proceedings. It would be hard for Joan to open up again, but Bishop Peterson fortified Joan's testimony of her religious beliefs. The man played a strong role in both David's and Joan's lives. Joan's faith in him was warranted. Through telephone conversations I learned to respect the man as a servant of God. He lived the principles.

On October 15, 1977, Joan wrote the following letter to Mark:

Mark,

I am writing to inform you of a new address and phone number for you to use when you want to make arrangements with me to see David. Just write or call Ken Peterson. (Here Joan listed his address and telephone number.)

As per instructions of the May 4, 1977 letter, send the money to help support the baby to the above address. You are now only $1350.00 delinquent on David's support. I am sure this is just an oversight on your part as your integrity and honesty are widely known.

Apparently you are still selfish and immature as ever... Oh, well, I'd much prefer to be paid directly by the court or your employer. And when I have this changed, I will also require a cost of living increase to keep up with inflation.

Joan

P.S. Had any raises lately?

In the event that Mark ever wanted to see David, it would be easier to arrange a time through Bishop Peterson who was living in the same area, than through Joan's brother Charley who had since moved to Texas.

During this period whenever Joan had two or three days free, we encouraged her to come and stay with us, rather than be alone with David in Colorado. Once, a few days before

Thanksgiving, she came to stay for a week. She brought with her copies of the will Byron Fisher had drawn up at her request and asked me to read it and offer suggestions or corrections. I had only one. Instead of paying out all the money to David at age 21, I thought it would be more circumspect to give him only part of it, then the remainder at age 25. A young man with too much money might be tempted to feel complacent and not finish his education. But the added incentive of an inheritance at 25 would add purpose to his goals and he would be more mature in handling such funds.

Joan liked my suggestion. She herself had felt that change needed to be made. She met with Byron Fisher for this purpose.

Some weeks later Joan brought in a letter to my office. She said that inside was one of the two original copies of her will. She asked if I would put one in my safe. I didn't read the will and so I was not aware of its contents. I merely assumed that she had changed the age to 25 as I had suggested. She asked if I wanted to read it, but I said no. It was not until many months later that I pulled out the will and read it.

I was not surprised that Joan had left Shauna out of her will, nor was I surprised to see that she had treated Virginia Kohtz the same as her sister Gail and her brother Charley. Although she and Virginia were not actually related, they had been like sisters and they felt extremely close. Virginia's father had passed away and Leone had married C.W., yet Virginia had always sent Christmas presents not only to Charley and Gail, but also to Shauna and Joan. She treated them all as if they were family.

In March of 1978, Joan brought me a letter. "Uncle Stan, I would like you to put this in your safe in the event that anything happens to me. Read it before I seal it."

I thought she was following Byron Fisher's instructions and had written out a list of her personal effects. I told her I would rather not read it, and I suggested that she seal it and write across the seal in two places.

I later learned that although she gave me this letter in March, she had actually written it on January 23rd. This was the letter that opened a Pandora's box after Joan's death. If she had foreseen the troubles it caused, would she have acted any differently? I doubt it. Joan knew what she was doing. She also knew her relatives and her former husband, their motives and their greed. She was trying to protect little David, making provisions for him before her death.

Early childhood. Joan and her Mother "Leone".

Growing up. "The youngest of four." Top, left to right: Gail, Charley. Bottom, left to right: Joan, Shauna.

Graduation from Bountiful High School, 1960

Graduation from Stewardess School, August, 1964 Joan: Front row, third from left

> May God be with you in these hours of grief...and may you have the faith to accept and trust His Will.
>
> We were on the flight—and Joan's calmness, efficiency and peace-filled Soul gave us strength..., as well as God's presence. We hope that you can find comfort in knowing that her life ended in giving to others. She displayed great comfort—and knowledge.
>
> We have her—and you in our prayers. We wish that we could give you a big hug...So we are asking God to do it for us.
>
> Sincerely,
>
> Jerry + Mary Clark
> &
> Laura Dwyer

Expression of sympathy and commendation from a family aboard ill-fated Jetliner.

Victim Honored

JOAN N. WHEELER

A Distinguished Service award has been given posthumously to Joan Newton Wheeler, 36, a former Bountiful resident who was first flight attendant aboard a United Airlines DC-8 that crashed near Portland, Dec. 28, 1978.

MRS. WHEELER was one of 11 persons killed when the plane crash landed near the Portland International Airport after experiencing landing gear problems. The majority of the 177 passengers escaped.

The award from the Federal Aviation Administration said of Mrs. Wheeler, "On her own initiative she led four other flight attendants in taking precautionary procedures for an emergency landing. Although killed in the ensuing crash, her professional dedication to duty helped save many of the 173 passengers who survived, and warrants the appreciation of all who fly."

THE CITATION and a medal were received by Mrs. Wheeler's uncle, Stanley C. Mann of Salt Lake City. Mr. Mann, executor of her estate, said he will hold the award for Mrs. Wheeler's 5-year-old son, David.

Mrs. Wheeler was a graduate of Bountiful High School, attended the University of Utah, BYU and worked in Washington before becoming a stewardess. She was born in Bountiful, the daughter of Charles W. Newton and Leoné Mann Newton. Both of her parents preceded her in death. She was living in Englewood, Colo. at the time of her death.

Final remains of Jetliner #173 which crashed 6 miles short of Portland International Airport on December 28, 1978.

Chairman's Award presented by Dick Ferris, Chairman of United Airlines.

ABOVE: Federal Aviation Administration Distinguished Service Award presented: "In recognition of her courageous leadership and exceptional performance prior to the crash of a DC-8 near Portland International Airport on December 28, 1978. Responsible for all cabin activities as First Flight Attendant, on her own initiative she led four other Flight Attendants in taking precautionary procedures for an emergency landing. Although killed in the ensuing crash, her professional dedication to duty helped save many of the 173 passengers who survived, and warrants the appreciation of all who fly."

LEFT: Federal Aviation Administration Distinguished Service Award Medal.

David attired in clown Halloween costume made by Joan for Halloween, 1978.

David. Age 3 years, 9 months. Christmas, 1978, at Grandma and Grandpa Mann's.

The Stigma of Divorce

After she made out her will, Joan started to have a better outlook on life. She still suffered from depression and times of self doubt, but she seemed more cheerful and able to look on the humorous side of things.

One night she called us from one of the cities where she was staying and we all had a good laugh at an experience she related. Men who tried to date her were often married, particularly the men on the crew. She had just checked into her room that evening when a knock came at the door. She opened it and there stood the first officer of the crew she was flying with. He stood there with his pants down, his genitals completely exposed. He smiled confidently, commenting that he knew she was divorced and hadn't been with anyone for quite a while. He was there to offer himself.

This was not an isolated instance. She had a lot of experiences which indicated that men felt divorced women were easy prey. Some even thought they were doing the divorced woman a service! Things like that didn't help her outlook, as concerned as she was about providing a home for her son with the type of environment that her religious upbringing demanded.

Besides the emotional aspects of her life, Joan suffered a financial stigma because of her divorce. She had difficulty establishing a clean credit rating after her divorce and she was still feeling the effects of Mark's bad credit on the Porsche.

The finance company even threatened a legal action against her. The car was Mark's, exclusively, a macho image, I suppose—but they were trying to hold Joan responsible for his debts. And every time she went to buy a house, she ran into a block—single women were not good credit risks, it seemed, despite the fact that she earned good money and had paid most of the bills when she and Mark were married.

She had plenty to contend with, but she was making headway. Probably the biggest single influence in reversing Joan's outlook toward the future was her bishop, T. Ken Peterson. After investigation, he felt that Joan had been done a terrible injustice. He recommended that she write a letter to the President of her church. A personal piece of correspondence, it reveals the strong yearnings of Joan's soul and explains the devastation brought upon her by one she loved and sacrificed for. She had turned the other cheek, again and again, only to be used and manipulated by Mark until she was crushed and almost broken.

I am in a position to know all of the injustices she endured, even by men in positions of leadership in her church who fell down in their responsibilities, some who actually lied in written communication about what happened between Joan and Mark. But never once did Joan say anything other than to confirm the last paragraph of the following letter.

April 6, 1978

President Spencer W. Kimball
50 East North Temple Street
Salt Lake City, Utah 84150

Dear President Kimball:

My husband, Mark Wayne Wheeler, and I were married June 9th at Annapolis, Maryland. From there, we drove directly to Salt Lake City and were sealed in the temple June 23rd, 1966. This brings me to the reason for this letter—to ask your permission for the cancellation of this sealing. We were divorced in Los Angeles August 23, 1976.

Over the ten years of marriage, there were long and constant separations beginning with the Navy and Viet Nam and continuing throughout to civilian life and his work. Mark was always immature and seemed to me to expect success and money overnight. He was constantly dissatisfied and changing jobs. (five jobs in five years).

During the last year of our marriage, we adopted a beautiful baby boy from the Social Services. Everything seemed to be going so well for us. We were both active in the church and Mark had just been called to a stake mission. At this time Mark told me that he was under a great deal of pressure at work and that things were not going well on his present assignment and there was a December 15th deadline. Mark was a little strange and irritable—on December 19th, 1975 we took our son to court in Los Angeles and finalized the adoption. When we arrived back home that morning, Mark announced he was leaving us and drove away with this thought, "Why won't you leave me alone so I can go out and kill my dragons?" He would not give me or the bishop a phone number or address. The bishop called Mark at work and over the next few weeks made three different appointments with him which he failed to keep. About three or four weeks later, I spoke with Bishop Price on the phone and he told me that he had finally talked with Mark, that Mark wanted a divorce and for the Bishop to tell me as he wouldn't face me. He also wanted to take our son to the temple still and have him sealed to us. The Bishop explained to him that was not possible.

Months passed and I found out that he had been involved with a girl at work, Miss Sylvi Ingebrigtsen (sic), and that he was using drugs and that he had been drinking secretly for the 13 years that I had known him. Many ugly things came out at this time.

I should also point out that he left me on another occasion back in April of 1973. At that time we were moving from New Jersey back to California. While driving along he very coolly announced that he didn't love me anymore and then drove to the airport in Chicago where he left me and caught a plane to the coast. He instructed me at that time not to tell anybody. After being gone a little over two weeks he decided he wanted to come home. Shortly after this I found out that he was seriously involved for five years with a married woman, Mrs. G. T.*, an old friend of his and that there were others. Mark insisted that they had only held hands and talked us all into believing it. A Bishop Ensign Call told me about this same time that he believed Mark to be bi-sexual. So many things happened and were so horrible I somehow put them out of my mind. At this point we moved into a new ward and went to the Social Services for counseling for a year.

It was always very hard to get Mark to discuss a problem and it was his practice never to admit anything that was not already known. One day he dropped by the house and told me that all his involvements with other women were never on a conscious level and that he missed us and the house. I tried to talk to him about the temple and our family and his reply was that the temple meant more to me than it did to him and he could always repent if he wanted to. I have wondered so many times now just who the real Mark is or was and what in our marriage was real?

The entire months we were separated before the divorce, he would bring his girl friend by our home every weekend. He was constantly telling me that I was crazy—many times I wondered if he wasn't right. On one of his rages he came out to the house in the middle of the day and kicked in the front doors. Then just a little over three months after he remarried, he came by the home to visit one evening and talked constantly about how happy he was now and how much better everything was for him. Suddenly he began to cry and crossed the room to me and tried to put his arms around me, explaining that he wouldn't hurt me. I told him to go home. Mark made sure that I suffered practically every humiliation possible.

I feel I should be granted a cancellation because he has broken his temple covenants; removed his garments; abandoned me twice; committed adultery; was dishonest and has lied for years; defrauded family and friends of money; cursed and threatened me on several occasions including in the name of the Lord, etc. Mark refused from the very beginning to give me any financial help or support. On top of this he has failed to provide any support for his son for over a year. His attitude was that it was the church's responsibility and then my family's to take care of us. I was married to a fraud.

In all the time since I first went through the temple for my endowments, I can never remember violating my covenants or my marriage vows. To this very day I still don't know how or why this nightmare ever happened in my home. This end was not the kind of marriage that I thought I had or the eternal life that I was striving to obtain.

In seeking this cancellation, I cannot see any possible chance for our marraige to continue. Mark has adopted completely different ideas and life style and I am of no value to him. I also believe it very possible that he is a true, devious, pathological liar. There are no plans in the near future to remarry.

President Kimball, I know that you are a true prophet of the Lord, and with all respect, I pray that you will take this request under your consideration.

Sincerely,

Joan N. Wheeler

(*Name purposely deleted.)

Although this letter was written on April 6th, Joan handed it to Bishop Peterson and he wrote a letter to accompany it some time later. On Tuesday, July 11th, about 1:30 in the afternoon, Joan called Louise at home. There was a ring in her voice that we had not heard for some time. She had just picked up her mail.

"Guess what? I just got a letter from President Kimball!" She read:

Dear Sister Wheeler,

In response to your petition I have this day cancelled your temple sealing performed in the Salt Lake Temple on June 23, 1966, between you and your former husband, Mark Wayne Wheeler from whom you have been divorced.

I trust that this action will pave the way for you to build solidly on a foundation that will continue to make your life acceptable to your Heavenly Father.

She was so excited that she asked Louise not to tell me; she wanted to call me herself. I cannot tell you the effect of this action on Joan. Anyone observing the change in her and her attitude would understand Joan's convictions and expectations. The stigma had been lifted.

At this point something else happened. Joan had a telephone introduction to a man, also divorced, who lived in Ohio, and Steve came out to meet Joan. They went out and had a fabulous time. At 2:15 in the morning my phone rang and I heard details of this date, almost moment by moment, step by step. It was one of the few long conversations in the middle of the night where I did not pass the telephone to Louise. I paid close attention.

This friendship grew and they telephoned and occasionally corresponded, and although he eventually married someone else, he restored Joan's faith that there were men in this world who held the same values that she did and lived by them. He was in the same circumstances as she, but he believed in a great future ahead. He treated her like an equal and confirmed her belief in the standards she had always tried to uphold. This man had an uplifting influence on my niece, and I am deeply grateful to him.

At this point Joan felt that it would be possible for her to return to California to live. She planned to use a bishop's name as contact for Mark and with an unlisted telephone number, she could keep her actual address and phone from getting into Mark's hands. She started looking for a house to purchase, and eventually decided on a home in Canoga Park.

This really gave her something to look forward to. She would be able to get back on the Los Angeles-Hawaii run with a turn-around schedule which would allow her to work days only, and only ten or twelve days per month at that. She put her home in Englewood, Colorado, up for sale. As the time came for completion of the California home, the house in Colorado had not been sold. The realtor arranged for her to get a bridge loan, the sum of which was in excess of her equity. It also tied her up to the point that if she listed the house with anyone else, the loan could be called in. The interest rate was substantially higher than the going rate.

All of these factors put Joan in a financial bind. On the

advice of friends in Colorado, she instigated suit against Mark to collect $4,500 in back support money. He had not paid one cent since she had deducted two months' support money from the $20,000 check she gave him as his share from the sale of their house.

Joan filed papers on December 16, 1978, the day before she came home for Christmas holidays, and told me about the suit when she first arrived. She regretted having to take this action because she was afraid that Mark would retaliate against her or David in some manner. Throughout their marriage that had been his practice whenever things didn't go his way. His favorite saying was, "There. Now you know what will happen if you ever do anything like that again." Their divorce hadn't changed his thinking. She wouldn't have filed suit if she hadn't been strapped financially.

Usually she saved up three weeks or so for vacation at holiday time, but this year she sold fourteen days of her flying time in order to get some money. She would be flying another flight attendant's schedule for the next three days. I took her back to the airport on the night of the 19th and David stayed with us, visiting with his Aunt Gail for two days.

Joan returned on Saturday, the 23rd, and we all went shopping and took David to see Santa Claus. We made final preparations for Christmas. On the 24th, David wrote Santa a letter and left it with a glass of milk and a plate of cookies. It was a great Christmas and we enjoyed ourselves to the limit. We took pictures, ate, and played games, and had a lot of fun. A real family-centered Christmas holiday. It was the last we would ever have with Joan and David. I'm glad we didn't know it then.

On the 27th, Louise and I came home from work to find dinner cooking and the house all vacuumed and dusted. Joan convinced a reluctant Louise that she could give her a home permanent without disaster and the girls got right at it after dinner. A short time later I heard uncontrollable laughter coming from the kitchen. Joan had gone into the utility room and heard something fall behind the dryer. She asked Louise if she had left a magazine or something on the dryer. Louise answered that she hadn't, but Stan had some seedlings sitting there in planting cartons. A few minutes later Louise found Joan practically standing on her head trying to retrieve my seedlings. When Louise inquired what on earth she was doing, Joan answered, "Saving my happy home!"

Her happy home is still here, but Joan cannot come home any more. Neither can her boy. But we are so grateful that we had them with us that last Christmas. Memories of those you love never diminish with time. They simply grow fonder.

A.D.: The Fight Begins

While I was in Denver attending to Joan's personal possessions and the disposition of her home, I went to the United Airlines Personnel office near Stapleton Field where Marilyn McArthur examined Joan's insurance papers with me. No one could have been more helpful or understanding than Marilyn. In representing her employer, she was the epitome of compassionate concern.

No one had ever moved Joan's car from the airport parking lot. Furthermore, since her keys and other personal items were never recovered at the time of the crash, I could only guess which one in the handful of odd keys I found at her house would fit the car—if we could even locate it. Marilyn helped me.

We went up and down the rows of cars and finally I spotted a red Firebird Pontiac halfway down the row. I tried a couple of the keys in my hand and one worked. The battery was dead, as I expected, but Joan always kept a set of jumper cables in her trunk and we used them to get the car started.

While we were waiting for the car to warm up, I looked in the trunk. Sure enough, there was the suitcase I had loaned her to bring back David's Christmas clothes that had to be exchanged.

The car ran terribly rough. A man had run a stop sign and smashed into Joan some months before, and she had gone through a terrible hassle, not only with her own insurance company but also with his. The other driver was cited for drunk driving and running a stop sign. Joan's insurance company should have taken care of everything; instead, they just ignored her. They even ignored a phone call from me. They would not have treated her that way if she hadn't been a single woman. They felt they could get away with taking no action on her case. The car had never run right since the accident, and sitting there in the parking lot certainly hadn't helped it.

I drove back to the house in Englewood and called the real estate agent who listed the house. When he arrived he hastened to inform me that they had received all kinds of inquiries about the house since the crash, but that those who had gone through in those first few days had been curiosity seekers, apparently, because nothing ever came of it. We talked about the price of the home and what could be done to facilitate a fast sale. I let him know that Joan had been disappointed in his activity in showing the home, and I wondered how he could stimulate traffic.

When I started to make inquiries about the company he worked for, he interjected, "Well, I was the one who got the bridge loan for Joan, and if you were to take the listing to anyone else, the bridge loan would be called in immediately." He asked if I had talked with any other real estate people. I hadn't, but I had been given the name of another firm who might get quick action for me, and my informant even mentioned the name of a sharp agent with that firm. The man left, but within an hour he called back. If we would leave the listing with him, he would be willing to give 10% of his commission to my church. That had no bearing on the matter, I told him. My only concern was in handling the matter the way Joan had designated.

Early that evening an attorney who had done some work for Joan came over to meet with me. He was aware of the bridge loan and Joan's financial circumstances. He advised me to walk away from the deal since the amount owing on the house would be in excess of what we could get from the sale, once the realtor's commission was paid. I would not do that and I told him so. Even if we had to take money from the house in California when it was sold to cover the deficit on this house, we would have to do it, for I would not compromise Joan's integrity or diminish her principles.

Because of high interest rates, as well as high payments, it was necessary to sell the house as soon as possible. (It ended up that we were over $11,000.00 short of meeting the mortgages when the sale was finalized!)

The next morning Bishop Peterson and I went to the airport to meet Louise and David. We felt it was important that David see the empty house so that he would know his mother was not there. We hoped this would help in his adjustment.

When Louise and David walked off the plane, Bishop Peterson held out his arms and David shouted, "Hey, where have you been?" The boy ran to him and jumped into his arms. It was obvious to everyone watching that this man had played a large part in the boy's life. I knew that the rapport and love he had demonstrated with Joan had affected young David's life, too.

Louise and I stayed in Joan's home for two days, going through as many things as we could that Joan had not already packed for the move to California. Part of the time we were there, David played outside with his neighborhood friends and we had to stop and play with them. Each evening we played games inside the house, David's favorite being the foos-ball dartboard. We had a lot of fun. On the second day, David came in with the news that one of his playmates said his mother was killed in an airplane crash. We prepared ourselves for a barrage of questions, but his only comment was, "I'll bet it smashed a lot of trees when it crashed."

The first night in Englewood David wanted to sleep with Louise and me. Three people in one bed. Not very restful. The next night we pointed this out to him, and he suggested helpfully, "Grandma can sleep in my bed." He revelled in a personal relationship with a man he figured belonged to him. There was no doubt that he loved his Grandma, but he wouldn't let Grandpa out of his sight.

I became greatly concerned over the way Byron Fisher had handled the custody matter, and when I found out that he had given Mark's lawyer a copy of Joan's will as well as her personal letter, I was really upset.

On our return to Salt Lake, I had several telephone messages, most of them long distance. One was from Colorado, two from Portland, all from complete strangers. The story was the same from all three. They knew of a lawyer who specialized in wrongful death actions and wanted me to talk with him before I made any other plans. I thanked each of them but said I had not given this matter a bit of thought and did not think I would for some time. There were too many other things to concern me at this point. Later that week an attorney from California called me for the same purpose. I told Byron about it and he advised me to seek out such an attorney, and to do so quickly before Mark could file through his attorneys. Byron had learned that Mark's attorney, Wayne Wadsworth, had just filed papers to put aside the temporary custody (which Judge Durham had approved for Louise and me) so that David could be turned over to Mark immediately. Part of their motion was based on the fact that Byron's procedure in the custody matter was faulty, and was therefore null and void.

I knew what this was all about. Mark felt that if he could get David, he would be able to control the trust funds. Later action confirmed this. Wayne Wadsworth's wife turned out to be the sister of Mark's new wife. Shauna's husband Dave Young was also working for Mark. That explained the calls to United and to the coroner in Portland.

I realized I was in for a real fight if I were to carry out Joan's wishes. The vultures were closing in for the kill. I was a fighter and I would not give in easily, but no way could I anticipate the nightmare I was heading into. I was on the threshold of an experience that would almost completely destroy my confidence in our judicial system. I can now best describe it as a tax-supported circus with more rings than Barnum and Bailey, and judges whose behavior would be interpreted as sick were it viewed in surroundings other than the courtroom.

I had related justice and law. I was soon to learn that the law holds very little relationship to justice, that no one has less respect for justice or the law than lawyers. Lying and perjury were regular and daily occurrences in courtrooms, and neither the lawyers nor the judges took any action against it; in fact, they did not even seem to notice it. Because they are officers of the law, they consider themselves above telling the truth, as if they are not accountable for justice. Even President Jimmy Carter says, "Americans are suffering from a crisis of confidence in our American system."

I would soon become well acquainted with lawyers. A bitter and slanderous personal attack would be launched against me, all because of my attempts to carry out Joan's will. I was the victim of both lies and innuendos. I shouldn't have been surprised at Wadsworth's doing these things. He had good training; he was a former F.B.I. man, and I knew from recent disclosures that F.B.I. men were well trained in dirty tricks.

Lawyers do not consider it lying, misleading or dishonest

when they act in this manner. They think they are absolved from the laws of integrity which you and I accept for our own standards. To them, their oath as a lawyer intimates that their position is to get their clients off the hook even if they are guilty as sin and dangerous to society, to boot.

This is where our legal system and justice are incompatible. They have grown completely out of proportion. Lawyers gain status in their profession by lying and misrepresenting the truth. They use technicalities to defeat justice, caring not at all for principles but acting only for their own glory—and for the money they receive from defending a client, no matter how guilty he is or how unscrupulous the situation.

Our legal system has grown into a morass devised to glorify actions which cause this crisis of confidence in our American system, and this, in my opinion, is the most dastardly enemy we face today, either inside or outside our country.

I had pledged myself. Now I would see it through, no matter what happened. Passionately, I felt the need to see justice conquer over all the treachery, scheming, malice and vindictiveness aimed at my poor niece. I would see it through! I wouldn't know how it was to end, but I planned to give it my best shot.

Legal Chicanery

I finally concluded it was necessary to bring in a lawyer who specialized in custody matters. Byron wasn't pleased, but I asked him to check around for the top custody lawyer in the Salt Lake area. I re-emphasized that he have no communication with either Dave or Shauna Young.

Because of the immediacy of the upcoming hearing it was agreed that he would call me back with suggestions for another lawyer. He called, but only to try to talk me out of engaging another attorney.

I contacted several people and asked them to give me the names of three top custody lawyers in Utah. Two names appeared on all three lists. I called Byron and asked if he had heard of Paul Liapis. He had. He agreed that Liapis was a fine lawyer. He would telephone Paul and make an appointment for 2:00 that afternoon. We agreed to meet in my office as most of the files were kept there.

At 2:00 o'clock Byron showed up—alone. He spent 45 minutes trying to talk me out of getting another attorney. He had not contacted Mr. Liapis. I was irritated. The hearing was scheduled for the next day, and Byron had ignored my instructions until it was almost too late.

I told him that if he didn't want to call Paul, I would. Byron assured me he would contact Liapis. He did and we had an appointment the next morning, the day of the hearing.

We asked to have the hearing postponed so we would have time to prepare our case and secure expert witnesses. This was denied. Mr. Wadsworth made patently false and libelous statements about me personally, unfounded accusations he knew nothing about, but he supplied evidence that the whole approach Mr. Fisher had followed was contrary to the normal procedure, and this was responsible for the refusal in delay.

The hearing was held on January 12th. Wadsworth, stood up and made blatant statements—lies—and Judge Bryant H. Croft followed with: "I think this is a most unusual situation, and I think that it is primarily a legal question, and while the best interest of the child may be a factor in certain guardian proceedings, I'm not satisfied that it is a factor that is present here to affect the legal decision that must be made here."

I could not believe my ears. The judge was saying, in effect, that the child's well-being was not an issue, that the law must be served, no matter what the cost to the child's future. He went on to say that Mark had tried to visit and contact the boy. That was an absolute falsehood, yet with no witnesses to corroborate our stand—the judge refused to allow any testimony—how could he arrive at a finding of fact? A totally incompetent decision!

Later I learned that this judge had reversed a jury who found a man guilty of rape. He turned the man loose with the memorandum that the act was "invited rape." What is "invited rape"—or "invited assault"—"invited robbery"—or "invited murder?" As I should have suspected, like Wadsworth,

Judge Croft was an ex-F.B.I. man.

Croft did one thing: he made Mark Wheeler post a $2500.00 bond, guaranteeing that he would bring David back for a full hearing on the matter of permanent guardianship at a future date. I felt that he did this because he felt uncomfortable with his decree. Maybe not. Who am I to judge the conscience of another man?

Wadsworth insisted that we turn David over to them under the auspices of the court and in the courthouse. I refused. I was not going to take a frightened little boy to a strange place and turn him over to a perfect stranger. Mark had to come to our home to get David.

The next morning I told David that his father had heard about the plane accident and wanted to see him. David said, "My father is a sheriff."

"No," I told him. "Your father works with computers."

Several times that day we told him his father was coming to prepare him for Mark's arrival. Beverly and Kerry Heinz and Gail and Glen came to offer moral support.

When Mark came, Wadsworth was with him. We invited them in and I introduced David to his father. The boy was completely indifferent. It was apparent that he wanted nothing to do with Mark. As we sat there in our livingroom, I suggested that David show his father some of his things, and we sat and conversed while Mark and David played on the floor.

Mark asked David if he remembered several things they had done together. The boy looked blank and answered, "No." Mark was a total stranger to him.

Several times I tried to bring Mr. Wadsworth into the conversation but he was cold and rude to everyone during the entire visit.

As time went on, Mark said, "Come on. David, Let's go have a pizza." David did not want to go. We had packed David's clothing and toys beforehand, and stacked them in the hallway. Wadsworth took the bags out to the car while Mark tried again to get David to go with him. Finally, Mark picked the boy up physically and carried him out of the door, kicking and screaming in protest.

We stood and watched them go. Our minds were empty; we couldn't think, we could only feel. But afterwards our friends said we should have won an Academy Award for our performance. We let David go with stiff upper lips and painted smiles, when all the time our hearts were breaking for the little fellow's anguish. Life would go on, but at that moment we didn't know how. My mind touched on the temptation I had felt a few days before when I knew that David would be taken from our home. For the briefest of minutes I laid plans to take the boy away and hide him where no one could find him as Joan had requested. I couldn't do it. My respect for the law was too great. Besides, the court would surely reverse their decision once the father's abandonment of the child was made known. This separation was only temporary.

But at that time I'd had little experience with court procedure.

Since that time David has had no contact with anyone he previously knew. A number of people have called the Mark Wheeler residence and asked if they could talk to David, or if their children could play with him. In each case the answer has been an outright refusal. They said David's pediatrician-psychiatrist had instructed that the child was not to see or talk with anyone he was familiar with.

On David's birthday we tried to talk with him. Mark answered the phone and when he found out who was calling, he denied he was Mark Wheeler.

When I was in Los Angeles regarding the court hearing Joan had instigated for David's back support money, Mark refused to let me see David or even talk to him.

Knowing from past experience that Mark would do anything for money, I made him an offer at the Van Nuys Courthouse. I told him I knew of his financial situation, that he had been unemployed since being fired from Sunn Classics, and that I would be willing to give him a substantial sum of money to help him out of his bind if he would turn David over to us. I made this offer because I knew he wasn't interested in David. He was interested in David's trust.

I went on. "Mark, I could sell some stock and have the money for you in a few days. How about thirty thousand within five days?"

He looked me coldly in the eye and said, "That's peanuts!" and walked away. There was no doubt in my mind that it was not the offer he objected to, it was the amount. It simply was not enough. Even then he was planning to overturn the trust and get control of it.

During this time, Wadsworth deluged us with letters making personal accusations against both Louise and me. He often referred to the material as coming from Shauna and Dave Young, but sometimes he made personal observations that were preposterous. The only personal contact we had with the man was in our home when we put forth every effort to make David's break as easy as possible, only to be rebuffed by Wadsworth's crude behavior at every turn.

One of the issues he brought up was David's bed. The inference was that David was attached to his bed and that we should send it to him, even though it was in Colorado. Wadsworth implied that, psychologically, it would be to the boy's interest if he were to be surrounded by familiar *things*, his toys, his clothes, his bed—but not *people*! I was dumbfounded. How could a smart man, an attorney, equate "things" with people?

Shortly after the bed incident I found that Byron Fisher had talked with Dave Young. He openly discussed matters of the will as well as the custody suit with him. He had even discussed coordinating in a wrongful death action against the airlines or the airplane manufacturer. This was a downright betrayal of my confidance and my instructions to him. It left me no alternative but to fire him.

I wondered why Fisher did this. He told me he had known Dave for a long time and he was an active member of the same church and a fine, upstanding fellow. How did that supercede a client's instructions, I asked? He had no answer. I found out that this fraternity of lawyers and their associations in most cases takes precedence over the client's interests.

On March 1st, Mark's deposition was taken by the attorney in Los Angeles who was trying to enforce the back support payment action. In this deposition Mark gave names and addresses of companies and individuals he had done business with, but when the papers came back, they did not acknowledge that they had dealings with him. In most cases they emphatically denied knowing a Mark Wheeler, yet Mark had given this information under oath! He also testified that he had made only $800.00 the first two months of that year, yet it was obvious from the home he was living in and by his life style that his overhead would have to have demanded an income of between $1,000.00 and $1,500.00 per month to meet normal expenses—and he had no visable income!

We learned that he had two, then three, and finally four unlisted phone numbers in his house, none of which were answered with "Wheeler residence." One number was an answering service, another The Instrumental Music Company. I have in my possession several tape recordings of Mark's voice answering this number. And, come to find out, this company—The Instrumental Music Company—had a non-existent address and the phone company had no address listed, just the phone number. The address, I learned, was a vacant lot several blocks away from Mark's home. Later, when a process server tried to serve papers on Mark and couldn't locate him, he called his number and got a recording: "This is the Instrumental Music Company. If you have an instrument you want to sell, please leave a description and your asking price and we will get back to you."

This raises many questions. Mark is a man who claims he is unemployed, cannot pay support money, gives names under oath of companies that he has done business with who deny even knowing him, has no visible means of support, yet lives in a home valued at about $240,000.00 with a large swimming pool, drives a Porsche and a large new station wagon—and he says he made only $800.00 during January and February combined of that year. This man has four unlisted phone numbers going into his house. What does it all add up to?

Immediately I recalled in Joan's notes where she said that Mark was involved with drugs. I wondered if this might be true. Even though it seemed extreme, other things she had told me about Mark proved to be true, why not this?

In the meantime my bishop had talked to Mark's bishop in California. He revealed that Mark and Sylvi planned on having Sylvi adopt David, then they would construe the meaning of the trust wherein it stated that if the guardians adopted David, they would receive the trust money. Joan had meant Louise and me, of course, but what did that mean to the law? Mark and Sylvi would get control of the trust, as I had suspected. After seeing our courts in action, I was not surprised at anything. The whole situation was unbelievable, yet I was forced to accept this possibility. I had seen too many things reversed by the courts.

In the middle of the month I called Morton A. Granas, Joan's attorney for the child support case against Mark. He had been unable to serve the papers for the judgment hearing on Mark. Every time the deputy went to the house he was told Mark was not at home—even though he had tried on evenings, weekends, and even Mother's Day.

The next day I heard through a long-distance phone call from MarJean Lewis that a few days earlier Mark had been shot four times in the chest by an unknown assailant. He was in the hospital in critical condition. (MarJean said that her friend was in hot water with her bishop for giving me a copy of her Ward directory, so she would appreciate it if I kept her name out of this. The reason I wanted the listing of Ward members was to verify the rumor I had heard that Mark and Sylvi named their new son "Mark." It was true. They had, and David's name was "David Mark." This led me to believe, even more strongly, that Mark really had no interest in David, nor did he even intend to carry on a relationship with the boy. If so, he certainly would not have named both of them after himself.) I inquired of some friends in that area to see if news of the shooting had been in the paper. They hadn't seen it. Neither had Mort Granas.

On Thursday the 17th, Virginia Kohtz called and said that two detectives had just left her place. They were interrogating everyone whose name appeared in Joan's will. It was routine. They assured her that Mr. Wheeler was "Mr. Clean" as they put it, and that the only difficulties he had were those involved with the custody battle over his adopted son.

They went on. Did she know that Mr. Mann had been in the Los Angeles area?

"Yes," she answered. "He stayed at our home two months ago and we were with him all the time he was here. If you're implying that he was mixed up in this shooting, you're barking up the wrong tree." Bless Virginia! She also informed them of some things she knew personally about Mark that kept him from qualifying for the Mr. Clean title.

They didn't give up. They asked the name of Joan's lawyer in California, and MarJean Lewis' address. They said they would be contacting all of those involved in the custody case and the will of Joan Wheeler.

On Monday morning, May 21st, Wadsworth filed an affidavit in Salt Lake City relative to Mark Wheeler's condition and the fact that he would be unable to appear on June 20th. The doctor's affidavit stated that it was doubtful that he would be out of the hospital by that time.

At approximately 1:30 P.M. on Tuesday, May 22nd, these same detectives from the L.A. Detective Bureau and Detective Jerry Thompson of the Salt Lake County Detective Division called me at my office and asked if they could speak with me. They came into my office, put a tape recorder on the floor, sat down and then turned the machine on. They briefly reviewed the shooting. When I let them know that I had heard about it before they had even called on Virginia, they asked me where I had received my information. I told them, but asked that they keep it confidential.

"Mr. Mann, could you verify your whereabouts on Friday, May 11th?"

Their question startled me because I was under the impression the shooting had occurred on Sunday or Monday following the 11th. I told them I could. I had been in this office and John Nicholson, my sales manager, and other office personnel would confirm that.

"Could each of your sons verify their whereabouts?"

This I didn't know for sure, but I imagined they could.

"What does your eldest son do, Mr. Mann?"

I told them he was a Utah Highway patrolman.

"And your second son?"

"He works at a ski lodge in Alta but is currently getting ready to go to Australia for the ski season."

They picked this up immediately. Was this a trip he had recently planned and when was he leaving? I informed them that he had been planning the trip since last Thanksgiving and would be leaving the early part of next month. This seemed to satisfy them for the moment.

"And what does your third son do, Mr. Mann?"

"He is a police officer in Draper, Utah."

They went back to the second son and asked more questions, specifically the date he was leaving and if he could verify his whereabouts on May 11th. Something unusual happened just then. The son in question happened to stop in at the office, something which rarely occurred. I motioned for him to come in and asked him the questions. He answered the first, then said he wasn't sure where he was on May 11th but he thought he was at home. "Why are you asking?" he wondered.

The detective then handed me a composite drawing of the assailant and asked if I had ever seen anyone who fit the description. That drawing came from a description given by Mrs. Wheeler. Then they gave me another drawing which they said came from Mr. Wheeler. Both drawings were of someone with a poor complexion and quite long hair. Then they pulled out a picture of a man who looked like he was tall, thin and malnourished. They asked if I had ever seen him, or if I knew him. I answered no.

They brought up some statements that Mr. Wheeler had made: first, that I was in Southern California at the time; also, that if he were dead I would get half a million dollars inheritance from his son, but that as long as he was alive, he would have the money.

I told them he was wrong on all counts. From my file I drew out my plane ticket stubs for my L.A. trips, gave them the dates and told them I had stayed with Virginia on this last trip, but I gave them the names and dates I had stayed at hotels.

I also straightened them out on a couple of other matters. Under no circumstances would Mr. Wheeler ever get hold of the money he was referring to. It belonged to David. He was mistaken. The total was approximately half the amount he told them, and the insurance companies had already paid off. I had some of the money in a trust and had partially invested the rest.

This was startling to them as it directly contradicted what Mark had said. I pulled out Joan's will and the trust and read them the paragraphs relating to the trustee. They asked for a copy of the document as well as the notes that Joan had left, which were to be used in the custody trial. I called Paul Liapis and asked if it would be all right to give them copies. He said it would.

I really wasn't too upset by the line of questioning. If I had been a suspect, they would have read me my rights. And I wasn't afraid to talk with them. I had nothing to hide.

The subject of Joan's notes concerning Mark's behavior while they were married came up and the detectives wanted to know the addresses of all the husbands of the women Mark had been going out with during those years. I didn't have them, but I expressed my willingness to share all the documents in my possession.

I asked why the shooting had not been in the newspaper. It had been kept out of the news, they told me, at the request of the Wheeler family.

"Mr. Mann, do you know anyone in any way connected with you who might take it upon themselves to go down and shoot Mr. Wheeler?"

Mark had given me enough difficulty over Joan's estate that I had reason to be upset. I told them that I did not know anyone who would shoot anyone for any reason, and as much as I had cause, I did not hate Mr. Wheeler. In fact, I had always liked him, but he was a compulsive liar and I knew from first hand experience that he did not care a rap for his son, that his only interest was in the boy's trust. Furthermore, I told them that he had used David several times to get money from Joan. He threatened, if Joan did not do as he asked, to go to the adoption agency and inform them that he and she had separated and that he had moved out before the final papers were signed for David. I could show them deposition papers which proved that Mark had perjured himself on numerous occasions. Then they asked if I could think of anything else or if anything else came up relative to Mark Wheeler or the shooting, or his connections with Sunn Classics, to please get in touch with them. I said I would. They left to go to Sunn Classics. I don't know what they learned there, or to whom they spoke, but it's a good guess that they learned of Mark's and Sylvi's connections with that firm.

Never in my wildest imagination did I ever think I would be questioned about an attempted murder. Before they left, the detectives asked me if I owned a handgun, and I told them I didn't own a gun of any kind.

My son corrected me later that night. "Dad, you do, too, own a gun. Remember, I'm under 21 and you had to sign for my gun, so technically, my gun is owned by you." He seemed pretty concerned about this so I told him not to worry about it. I assume they never ran a check on registration—or figured they caught me in a lie. At any rate, they never came back.

I related my experience to John, my sales manager, and he remembered something. "You know, Stan, that particular Friday is the only Friday I haven't been in the office since I started working for you. I took the day off for my daughter's graduation, remember?"

I heaved a sigh. What now?

But as John was leaving for the day, he came back to tell me that I had taken several calls from salesmen that day and the salesman from Pocatello had been late making his call into the office. He had reached me about 5:50 that evening. "Don't worry," John said. "I'm sure we can establish your whereabouts for each hour of the day."

Knowing how things can be twisted in the courtroom, I was relieved.

The events that have arisen over Joan's death become more bizarre by the day. I told the detectives all of Mark's unlisted phone numbers and gave them the numbers, but I don't think there was any follow-up. They also told me there was another witness besides Sylvi, a neighbor. At the time I didn't think anything about it, but now I wonder why they didn't have a composite drawing from her? And why they didn't show the drawings to Virginia Kohtz? They have never shown them to anyone involved in the custody hearing.—Nor have they questioned people in California or those persons named in Joan's will. They haven't even contacted the lawyer in California whose address and phone number they requested from Virginia. Why not? Have they solved the case? Was I the only one Mark pointed a finger at? I don't understand these things, and I need to, for David's sake as well as my own.

At the first of the interview with me they repeated the same thing they said to Virginia: "As far as we can see, Mr. Wheeler is Mr. Clean." Virginia told them differently, and so did I. I'm no detective, but this stuff smells to heaven to me. What kind of cover-up is Mark using? What kind of influence does he have?—Or is it Wadsworth's influence?

And where in the name of heaven is all of this going to lead little David and his loving grandparents who long more for him each passing day? Our prayers at night begin and end with the same thought. "Please, Heavenly Father, keep David safe, and in Thy infinite wisdom, help him grow up strong and healthy and happy in the path his dear mother wished for him."

More Chicanery

There was a lot of confusion about Mark's condition after the shooting. The police kept the entire matter from the press. No notice ever appeared in the papers and when my attorney asked for information about the shooting, it was refused.

I was frantic about David. Even though I had not heard about the shooting until Wednesday, May 16th, Wadsworth was fully aware of it. On May 14th he filed a request for protective order for the purpose of removing Mark's deposition from Salt Lake City to California in order to restrict severely any questions that might be asked. This act was obviously timed and engineered to hide the circumstances surrounding the shooting and to prevent inquiry into Mark's activities which might account for the supposed attempt on his life.

I use the word "supposed" purposely. A number of people who knew Mark suggested to me that this was the kind of thing he might pull to gain sympathy or attention. Never at any time did I—or my lawyer—entertain such a thought.

The subject was brought up by Wadsworth himself, but he added it was ridiculous to think Mark would do such a thing.

The detectives said that it was the request of the family to keep anything relative to the shooting out of the papers, but I am still amazed that police officers would collaborate in withholding news from the press, and I believe that Wadsworth, through his connections with the FBI, arranged the secrecy.

Dr. Thomas Conklin signed an affidavit on May 21st stating that he was one of the medical doctors who had been, and still was, responsible for the care and treatment of Mark W. Wheeler. He further stated that Mr. Wheeler was still hospitalized and in very serious condition. His release date from the hospital was unknown, but even if he should be released by June 20th (the date of the deposition), he would not be strong enough to travel. He stated that interrogation of Mr. Wheeler within the next 60 days would be very stressful and should be conducted with great caution.

We filed a response to the affidavit on May 23rd, agreeing to a postponement of the trial to give us time to prepare after Mark's deposition was taken. The hearing on this matter was held before Judge Dean Conder on May 25th, and when he disallowed the protective order but said he would grant a postponement in the taking of the deposition, Wadsworth stood up in court and reversed his own motion. After the protective order was refused, he said Mark would be in Salt Lake on June 20th for the taking of the deposition. They did not want a postponement but would go ahead with the dates that were scheduled!

My lawyer and I looked at Wadsworth in amazement. So did Judge Conder. But he said nothing. The issue was passed over as casually as if truthfulness were irrelevant in a courtroom. Later we found out from Mark's deposition, that he left the hospital the very same day that this motion was being ruled on by the judge.

About this time responses from the businesses Mark had claimed to have dealings with started to flood back in. In each case, they either denied doing business with Mark or knowing him, or both. Mark was a pathological liar, all right, just as Joan had suspected, but I wondered if this wasn't going a bit too far, even for him. He must have had some connection with these companies. Were they a front for some illegal activities, tied in, somehow, with his ununlisted phone numbers? The respondents would have to deny knowing Mark in order not to implicate themselves and to embroil their companies in an investigation. What next, I wondered?

I was soon to find out. Early in the morning, about 2:30 A.M. on May 31st, (approximately the same hour Mark called me at the time of Joan's accident) I received two mysterious phone calls. They both woke me out of a sound sleep, but I managed to say "hello" several times. No one answered. Each time, however, a sound like someone choking sputtered in my ears. I held the phone for several minutes, then hung up. Five or ten minutes later the same thing happened. The following week, on Wednesday, June 6th, I was working late at the office. A little after 6 P.M. the phone rang. A male voice said, "You had better watch yourself. We are going to get you." And he hung up. The next day on Thursday I answered the phone and heard the same choking sounds. This happened several times. Each time I was a little more unnerved than the time before.

At first I contemplated calling the police, but then I remembered a conversation with my attorney. He said one thing that might upset the court or worry the judge about leaving little David in Mark's custody was the fact that an attempt had been made on Mark's life. The boy's safety might be questioned. Perhaps this motivated my callers. They wanted it to be a matter of record that my life had been threatened, and that the boy's safety would be endangered if he were in my home. I decided not to report the incidents.

But the following day I gave instructions in my office. If anyone asked for me on the phone, the caller should be identified before I accepted the call. I was not going to pick up the phone under any circumstances unless I knew who was calling. This helped, but the calls continued. The following week John Nicholson took my calls several times. In each case no one answered. John heard only the familiar choking sound. The same tactics had been used on Joan and it had finally forced her to leave California. She wanted a semblance of a sane life without the threat of a vindictive man putting her into a state of panic.

On July 30th, while we were away from home, probably about 12:30 A.M., someone climbed up a pole where the telephone and safety systems for the three homes in my neighborhood were located, and tore out the wires for my home only. Then Louise started receiving obscene phone calls at the office. When anyone else answered, the caller hung up. It was a mature male voice, and Louise said it sounded familiar, but she would not identify it. However, Mark made similar calls to Joan after they were divorced and we had recordings of the caller at that time (although Mark denied it was he.) The voices sounded the same.

On Wednesday, June 20th, when Mark and Wadsworth came into Paul Liapis' office for the taking of Mark's disposition, we had the judgment papers for back support money served on Mark just as he entered the office. During the day, even while giving his deposition, he repeatedly perjured himself. Wadsworth fell into the same pattern, completely violating the oath which he took upon becoming an attorney. It was easy for me to see how Wadsworth and Dave Young had collaborated so well in legal matters, Dave having been cruel to the old (Shauna's parents) and Wadsworth to the young (little David.) It seemed neither of them had a drop of the milk of human kindness in their veins. Or respect for the truth!

In one of his letters, Wadsworth wrote that he had instructed Mark and Sylvi not to let David have any contact with his Grandma and Grandpa Mann. He ordered the isolation of a three-and-a-half-year-old child, torn away from everything and everyone he knew. Can you imagine the fear, the insecurity forced on a boy in this position? He probably thought he had been kidnapped—or abandoned. After all, he had lost his mother's mother, or "Ma," as he called her, only a little over a year before, and his mother only recently. Now his Grandpa and Grandma Mann were gone. No wonder David had to be drugged. I couldn't let myself dwell on the boy's state of being. It was so distressing I couldn't stand the thought.

But every time I thought of David, how this well-adjusted little boy had been dragged out of familiar and comfortable surroundings and thrust into a life which at best could be described as hell, I can only feel that Wadsworth, a reputably religious man, was possessed with greed.

Throughout this whole legal mess, Wadsworth repeatedly lied, slandered and attempted to mislead the judge through tactics which clearly violated his oath as an attorney. Lawyers apparently try to justify their action by use of the principle they refer to as "advocacy," but to my way of thinking, they use advocacy to hide or to justify violations of their oath or to cover actions which are dishonest and unethical.

If Wadsworth were taken before his state bar, the matter would be presided over by the chairman of the committee over ethics and discipline—and that man is a member of the same law firm as Wadsworth!

The legal profession and the judiciary caused the breach of public confidence in America and democracy. Does the Constitution or the Bill of Rights give lawyers rights that others do not have, or are we all equal? Is a lie a lie only when it is spoken by someone other than a lawyer? And is perjury perjury only when declaimed by someone outside of the legal profession? Apparently, a lawyer can commit perjury legally if he simply refers to himself as an advocate. Why should a lawyer, an officer of the court, be immune to slander or libel? No one has voted him into office, or even approved him as an officer of the court, nor has anyone had an opportunity to evaluate his performance or fitness for such a position.

Lawyers' self-proclaimed "advocacy" has been made into a catch-all justification for every moral and ethical violation anyone can lay a finger on. Where in the Constitution does it claim that lawyers and judges can perform their functions in secret behind closed doors and refuse the American citizen (who often has much at stake) the right to know what they are doing? Any honest, upright attorney or judge should welcome public scrutiny of his work and actions.

After showing Joan's will to several attorneys, I was advised by each of them that there was a clear case of malpractice against Byron Fisher. I showed them the documents surrounding the entire matter, her estate, the trust and the attempt by Dave Young to subvert Joan's will, even though he and his wife were involved in another entanglement which represented a conflict of interest, according to the Revised Rules of Professional Conduct for the Utah State Bar.

Since they had confirmed my feelings, I asked two of these lawyers if they would handle a case of malpractice as they had explained it to me. They declined. I asked another attorney, a member of an entirely different law firm, if he would be willing to take a malpractice suit against another attorney in Utah. The question made all of these professional men extremely uneasy. In various ways they answered that they did not feel experienced enough in that area, and when asked for the name of an experienced attorney, they refused any information on the grounds they did not feel it would be proper. I asked if they knew of malpractice suits against any attorneys in Utah. They declined to answer.

Is it any wonder that the legal profession is probably one

of the largest sources of white collar crime? We have allowed them to write their own set of ethics as opposed to that for the average citizen. We have also allowed them to conduct all of their own evaluations and to do so in secret. No individual is allowed to check to see if the attorney he might engage has a record of malpractice, a record of complaints against him by clients, or a record of fraudulent practices. Why not?—Because the Bar Association says if a rumor anything like that leaked out, the man's career would be ruined. Should lawyers be different from any other businessmen? Lawyers won't permit a rumor or complaint to be aired, yet they will blatantly justify falsehoods of their own, getting up in court, in public, and making a matter of public record false and unfounded statements and the bar takes no action. Furthermore, the judge sits there listening to such statements and does not even ask for evidence for such preposterous claims. No wonder the legal profession wants to keep the press, and especially television, out of the courtroom.

It is high time we disallowed a self-proclaimed elite to commit immoral and unethical crime as they hide behind technicalities. Those practicing law should be subject to the same scrutiny as other businessmen. The distinction in code of ethics which lawyers expect to be judged by is the same distinction which has been administered to those commonly referred to as blue collar criminals versus white collar criminals. These are double standards, unconstitutional, unconscionable and destructive to the confidence of the American people in so-called justice. The ramifications of this whole line of thought will be disastrous for our country and its citizens.

I have cited examples of only a handful of situations, yet I know—and I am prepared to substantiate—that many of these crimes are common in the legal profession today.

Other states are moving to correct the injustices which have been forced upon citizens by the legal profession in ever-increasing numbers. Utah is lagging far behind. Why are reputable members of the profession protecting the likes of a conspiring Wadsworth and Young? I sometimes wonder if the predominance of Mormon attorneys in this state might have spawned an inner circle, a fraternity as it were, which leads to scratching each other's backs. Whatever the reason, because of their greed in achieving the accoutrements of success (money, prestige, etc.), most of them seem to lack the backbone and character to take a stand in correcting obvious injustices perpetrated upon people. Professional bias might be the answer. If it is, then something must be done to check and balance these practices.

Piety and Perversion

From the things Mark Wheeler said to me after he talked to Byron Fisher about Joan's will and trust, I did not expect him to make any effort to get custody of David or control of the trust. After hearing parts of the will, he seemed to have all of the wind taken out of his sails. I believe the whole matter would have been dropped right then and there, had it not been for Wadsworth and Dave Young. There is no doubt in my mind that they incited Mark to action by telling him that in all probability he could gain custody of David, and if he did, there might be some legal technicality they could maneuver to subvert Joan's last will and testament, to break the trust and to get their hands on her money.

Dave Young's past activities indicate this kind of thinking. It was not the first time he acted in this manner. And Wadsworth—well, I found Wadsworth to be a classic example of arrogance, sanctimony, and crudity. He was capable of anything for personal gain. His lies, perjuries and misrepresentations in this area clearly categorize his character.

Despite their obvious record, both of these men parade around, piously proclaiming themselves to be practicing Christians. During the months I've observed these men in action, I often wondered how they answered their spiritual leader when he asked them, as all Mormons are questioned: "Are you completely honest in your dealings with your fellow men?" Does their conscience allow them to openly lie, or do they hide behind the rhetorical answer: "Yes, I am honest within the context of my profession." (I have been advised by several of these spiritual leaders that more and more lawyers are responding in just this manner. But even this can in no way justify their unethical or immoral behavior. I sometimes think it is no accident that—at least in Utah—the words "lawyer" and "liar" sound alike.)

Mark Wheeler didn't need to be coached by professionals. But the facts indicate that he was. He told the Los Angeles police that he was sure I was in L.A. at the time of the shooting and that I was the only one with reason to shoot him, that if he were not alive I would come into a large sum of money. All of this, of course, was patently false. First of all, I was not within 800 miles of the shooting: in fact, I was not even aware of the shooting until five days after it occurred since there was obvious manipulation to keep it out of the papers.

Second, I was not the one who would profit from someone's death. Mark would have a chance to profit from my death, if the situation were reversed, but what had I to gain? Obviously this was a bit of legal dealery. Wadsworth plotted to blame me in order to defame my character. He thought this would help them get their hands on the money, and I think he and Dave Young planned to discredit me in other ways. There was a robbery (so-called) and a forgery committed in Mark's neighborhood in California, they claimed, and they tried to blame both on me, but the interesting thing is that the persons involved were not at all certain the crimes took place. Wadsworth led the witness and misconstrued every answer he gave so as to make me look like the "heavy."

I could forgive him for that. What I couldn't overlook are his contradictions, his flagrant lies with regard to little David. He intentionally isolated a small boy who was just coming out of a state of shock, all for the sake of winning a case. Wadsworth repeatedly lied and contradicted himself in letters and documents to both Paul Liapis and the court as well as at the hearing in front of a judge. More than Mark Wheeler, Wayne Wadsworth is responsible for the emotional disturbance of the child, for he himself admitted, in letters and admissions, that it was *he* who ordered David's isolation from us and from everything else that was familiar to him.

David was examined and treated by a Robert H. Marshall, M.D., whose competence as a child psychiatrist is in question in my mind. The man prescribed tranquilizers and arrived at conclusions regarding the boy's condition and causes responsible for his condition after seeing the boy only two times, once in the office and the other when Sylvi brought in her baby for examination. Most of his findings about David evolved from statements made by Sylvi, not from his own observations. This man even drew conclusions about the personality and character of Joan Wheeler, a woman he never met, and about whom he heard only through the jaundiced eyes of Mark and Sylvi. As you might suspect, the doctor's deposition is filled with discrepancies, contradictions, and outright falsehoods.

Both Mark and Sylvi were concerned that David had become a perpetual liar. This accusation of theirs was startling in light of the fact that many who knew Mark realized that he was an inveterate liar. Even his family admitted that. But little David was never known to lie until he was carried screaming from my home. Perhaps this was the boy's adjustment to his new life. He certainly had a good model to follow.

In a few references from the transcript of the custody

hearing, Wadsworth interrogates Doctor Marshall.

QUESTION: "In your professional judgement, what would be the effect if the boy was moved from the care and custody of Sylvi at the present time?"

ANSWER: "I think it would be a disaster. She is the only person he can cling to and have any knowledge in his own mind that she will be there. She will be steadfast, give him love and affection, she will give him attention and she won't disappear."

QUESTION: "What do you feel would be the effect on David, given his anxiety at present, if there were a divorce between Mr. and Mrs. Wheeler?"

ANSWER: "If there were a divorce, it would be still another blow and it would be catastrophic."

QUESTION: "What would be your opinion in the event they were to separate, and Mr. Wheeler was to take David with him?"

ANSWER: "It is hard to really evaluate at this time as we would have to see what adjustment the boy makes, first, to the appearance of Mr. Wheeler in the house. Before the shooting I would have answered that he would be unhappy that Sylvi was gone, because this would still be another blow but that he would have made a pretty good adjustment with Mr. Wheeler, but at this time, I really cannot answer, because he had denied the existence of Mr. Wheeler at the time I had spoken to him. It is entirely possible that the adjustment would not be good, that he would prefer to be with Mrs. Wheeler."

In addition to other facts regarding Mark's relationship with Sylvi and their marriage, this worries me. Is Wadsworth laying the groundwork for Sylvi to adopt David? Sylvi is Wadsworth's sister-in-law, and in the event of a divorce it would be Sylvi who would get control of the trust money if the trust were broken. I believe Wadsworth is trying to protect Sylvi, knowing the past histories of infidelity on the part of both Mark and Sylvi, and realizing the failure rate of second marriages, especially marriages that start out on shaky footing such as this one.

Like Wadsworth, I would bet against this marriage continuing, but what he is preparing for, I am not certain. All I know is that David will suffer. Neither the doctor's report nor his faith in Sylvi's maternal instincts are reassuring to me. I am more frightened for David than ever before. Is any amount of money worth jeopardizing the future of a frightened, insecure child barely four years of age?

Birds of a Feather

Probably the main thing wrong with judges is that they were previously lawyers. The practice of law distorts a man's common sense more than any other experience in the world. Enough exposure to the lack of ethics and morality common to such a large majority of those practicing law today would pervert the purposes of many a man. Some of these men become judges. In many cases they not only hand out falacious decisions, they also usurp, legally, the perogatives and responsibilities of our legislatures. They hand out rulings not voted on by duly elected legislators such as school busing, secret trials, plea bargaining, etc.

Judges attempt to promulgate the image of the infallability of the judiciary. Our courts are fraught with contradiction and inconsistency to the point where a high percentage of our citizens suffer from a crisis of confidence in all things legal, not just in politicians. Some of the incompetent decisions and unfounded findings of fact by judges in Utah are disgusting. These are not just the work of the late Judge Ritter. The precedent continues.

Many judges are like the professional athlete who signed a no-cut contract. He became a self-centered and conceited man, thinking that he was "the greatest." When he assumed such an attitude, he stopped putting out his best efforts. Some judges act the same way. No one needs to go to the movies to see an enactment of the typical judge. You can go to any courtroom and witness the same sort of pompous, irresponsible behavior that sells theater tickets on the screen.

In 1978, Yankelovich & Skelly and White, Inc., a reputable research organization, was hired by the National Center for State Courts to conduct a survey to assess public image of the courts. Shortly after this survey was made, the Office of the Utah State Court Administrator engaged the Wasatch Opinion Research Corporation in Salt Lake City to conduct a survey of the same subject, but the Utah survey used an entirely different set of demographics for their study. As a result, although national courts come off poorly, as one would expect, Utahns seemed to approve of their state courts, even though the average man on the street is appalled at what goes on. The explanation? A restructuring of the questions asked, and the omission of other points of consideration, skewed results so dramatically that no conclusions regarding Utah courts could be reached. A comparison between the two studies was impossible. Who was in charge of the Utah study?—Judges, of course.

Judges become like politicians once they are in office. They take upon themselves knowledge of all things. They know what is the best disposal of your money, they know what you should have done or said in your last will and testament, and they assert their self-proclaimed authority to change whatever they deem proper, regardless of your intention. God help you if you are dead and cannot speak up for yourself! In effect, judges freely practice the art of violating your constitutional rights.

Just like politicians, judges seem to avoid hard decisions. It's easier that way. Some are spineless demogogs whose presence on the bench is not only demoralizing but actually a perversion of justice.

In the custody hearing with Judge Baldwin, in Utah's Third District Court, I was on the witness stand being cross-examined by Mark's attorney. He said, "Are you in effect accusing Mr. Wheeler of perjury?" I answered, "I am," and the judge immediately countered, "Strike that from the record. I won't have that kind of thing entered into in this court." No wonder several lawyers have declared that judges never do anything about perjury in a civil suit, and rarely in a criminal case.

In the same hearing, Judge Baldwin said, "Perjury and lying and non-support, abandonment not compelling or cogent, were not strong, serious or grave enough to be considered for this hearing." If he overlooks a man perjuring himself, how can he pass judgement on testimony given? How can he decide that a man is a fit or worthy parent if he is not moral enough to tell the truth? How can he make a serious decision on behalf of a child when he refuses to investigate the truth of any claims?

During the hearing the judge acted completely without dignity. He was uninformed about statutes he himself referred to. He cited examples and then when it came down to it, he changed the subject abruptly because it was obvious he couldn't follow through on the cases. Judge Baldwin ran true to form.

It isn't necessary to look at daily conflicts in national publications. The open misuse of judicial power, right here in Utah, is apparent every day. Third District Judge James Sawaya gave as a lame excuse for the sentencing of a recent rape case: "I am given no choice in this matter by the statutes." This decision involved a man who was presently serving a one-to-fifteen year sentence on another rape conviction and had escaped from a prison half-way house, kidnapped and repeatedly raped a sixteen-year-old girl. Judge

Sawaya remanded him into the custody of the state mental hospital. Personally, I think the prisoner knew what he was doing. He had done it before!

The excuse, "I am given no choice in this matter," used by weak judges, is so familiar that the public gets bilious every time they hear it. Another case heard by Judge Sawaya: a thirty-year-old Utah man had intentionally and systematically bilked over 300 people out of over one-half million dollars over a short period of time. He did not do this unintentionally or through bad judgment. He did it through greed and dishonesty. Originally he was charged with twenty-one counts of felony theft but through plea bargaining he was allowed to plead guilty to only one count. Judge Sawaya sentenced him as follows: "Never engage in such a business again, serve thirty days in jail during summer vacation from school and attempt to repay your victims." The judge put him on indefinite probation and ordered him to finish his education. This man is presently attending Stanford University. Those he bilked out of their savings, in sums ranging from $2,000 to $10,000, cannot afford to go to school or even meet their financial obligations in some cases.

In this case Judge Sawaya said justice was better served if the defendant were on the outside where he could pay the victims back. The judge used the excuse that the man came from a good family, that he had never had a prior arrest. The statutes do not state that penalties for crime can be altered if a man comes from a good family. To carry the matter further, what is a good family? Judge Baldwin implies that you can be a good family man even if you lie and perjure and abandon and commit adultery. He refused to go into any of the possible reasons why anyone might want to shoot Mark Wheeler. I want to know why a good family man would have someone out to kill him in cold blood? Shouldn't the judge be a little curious about this matter when he is investigating a home into which a small child will be placed?

In another case Judge Sawaya sentenced to jail for one year a nineteen-year-old boy who committed an offense when he was eighteen. He drank half a pint of whiskey on a bet, got into a car and was involved in an accident in which the other party eventually died. The judge convicted this boy of vehicle homicide. I cannot justify his act, but note that he was eighteen, not thirty, that he did not set out intentionally to commit a crime and he certainly had not plotted systematically to involve himself in an accident which would take the life of another human being.

What is the judge trying to say?—That this young man did not come from a good family? The thirty-year-old man was a descendent of a former governor of the state, he was Caucasian and came from a family long active in politics, civic affairs, and was a member of the dominant religion in the area. Maybe this is what classifies him as a "white collar" criminal, rather than a "blue collar" or common criminal. The common criminal is usually motivated towards crime for reasons of poverty, fear, feelings of inferiority, and sometimes passion, and to supply the needs of loved ones. "White collar" criminals generally commit crimes because of greed. These crimes are premeditated, preconceived, and plotted intentionally. Yet judges deal with the latter more leniently. There exists a double standard in the courts today. No wonder Utah is known as the fraud capitol of the country.

(A thought for consideration: possibly this high rate of fraud and "white collar" crime in Utah is related in some way to the high percentage of lawyers in comparison to the population along the Wasatch front. After all, lawyers are the champions of "white collar" crime, and in many cases the instigators of it.)

Near the end of the hearing, Judge Baldwin topped even his previous performance. He told the court reporter, "I want to go off the record." Then he proceeded to make a complete fool of himself. He didn't quite know how to act, he said, because he had two office holders of his own faith there in the courtroom and my attorney, Paul Liapis, who was of a different faith. Condescendingly, the judge proceeded to tell my attorney, who had been a gentleman throughout the whole repugnant procedure, that he probably did not quite understand the importance of the family and how it was held in the Mormon church. This was degrading. Paul Liapis was a conscientious lawyer who honored his oath of office with great dignity. The opposing attorney, our friend Wadsworth, had displayed one of the most demagogic performances I have ever seen, both before and during the hearing. And here the judge was carefully explaining their "higher" standards.

This type of behavior has no place in the courtrooms of Utah or any other state. Anyone who would take the position that Judge Baldwin had assumed, the contradictions and the lack of interest in getting at the truth of the matter with regard to the well-being of a small child, and then self-righteously infer that people of his faith hold their families closer and of greater importance than people of other religious beliefs—well, this was one of the most tasteless displays of arrogance I have ever witnessed in my life.

This was typical of the behavior I was to observe in the courtrooms in months to come. Was there any hope for my cause if my case were to be decided by clowns whose judicial posturing was of more importance to them than the dissemination of justice? Would little David ever find a home where he would be loved for himself, not for the trust that his mother had prepared so painstakingly for him? Would the boy ever inherit that trust?

These thoughts penetrated my mind until I wondered if I would go mad with worry. What in the name of God was happening to my country? What was it coming to when justice could be perverted even in defense of a helpless boy? Could I, his uncle, fight hard enough to secure his rights for him? My family had suffered, even now, for the stand I took. How much more would they have to endure before justice would be served? Did I have the right to foster this tension upon their heads? They supported me thus far but it seemed that the fight had just begun. How much more time, money, effort, legal battle and turmoil would be required to end this conflict of wills? Did I have the courage to do the job?

    I pounded the desk in anger. Yes! With all that was in me, by all the powers of justice and truth that I believed in, by the mercy of God Everlasting I would fight to my last breath. Joan expected it of me. David needed me. I would do the job. I would fight a good fight. To the end. Whatever the cost.

And So It Stands

Shauna, Joan's only full sister, had always treated Joan with contempt, and apparently she came to identify me with Joan, for as she grew older we didn't always get along. I tried to be as pleasant as possible under the circumstances, but I really didn't like the girl, especially after I learned how she had treated both Leone and C.W. It was bad enough while Joan was still alive, but after her death Shauna seemed to carry out her own personal vendetta against me. She tried me to the limit. Once, in a moment of grave trial I muttered to her, "Shauna, your greed spreads like a diseased whore."

Her vengeance knew no limits. Three days after we learned that Mark had been shot, I was contacted by my bishop. A General Authority of our church had telephoned him and asked, "What is this story I hear concerning this member of your ward who is implicated in an attempted murder?"

Police had previously contacted me and although I was personally shocked to think that they would give credence to any shaky finger of accusation Mark pointed at me, I answered all of their questions and they left, satisfied. I never saw them again. But Shauna and her attorney husband saw a chance to discredit me with church officials, and they lost no time in pursuing this course of action.

I was eager to clear myself, but it was several months before I could arrange an interview with the church leader. My stake president and my bishop, who was fully acquainted with the details of the family fracas, accompanied me to the church office building, along with my wife and my brother Charley who flew in from Idaho to be with me.

The interview went well. I felt completely vindicated of any involvement in wrong-doing, and the church leader assured me that if Shauna and Dave's purpose was to bring any church action against me in the custody or the trust fight, their plans had backfired.

I might not have been so certain of the source of all this malicious action if we had not caught sight of Shauna and Dave in their four-wheel-drive vehicle as we left the premises of the building after our appointment. They confirmed my deepest suspicions by pursuing a highly irregular route. They must have been circling the block. When we spotted them they were heading west. Suddenly they turned across the street into a closed parking area, pulled out abruptly into the middle of the block and headed east full speed to avoid us. They were involved, all right!

But I was relieved! The authorities of the church believed me. My conscience told me to continue the fight for justice, regardless of the consequences. Someone had to stand up for Joan, and it seemed that I was her only champion.

When the proceedings to determine permanent custody of David took place, on July 23, 1979, Mark Wheeler bungled badly—although none of us knew it at the time. Because incompetent Judge Baldwin was hearing the case, it was almost impossible to establish any line of questioning which would elicit information, but Paul Liapis tried. Finally even Baldwin seemed to tire of the circus. He turned to Mark. "How much do you make a month?"

Mark answered, "It varies. I give my wife $3,000.00 every month to take care of the house payment and bills."

The judge said impatiently, "What I am getting at are the income tax reports filed here. Is that indicative of your income?"

Mark answered, "Yes, sir, that is."

Both Wadsworth and Dave Young looked up suddenly, startled by Mark's answer. They were obviously disturbed by this disclosure.

The courtroom sensed the static in the air. No one moved. You could actually hear the silence. Mark had perjured his own testimony given in California with regard to his financial status.

Paul followed this revelation with the statement, "With regards to his income and how it relates to his business, or excuse me, his home expenditures, we have not had that information, and quite frankly, to answer your questions, we have no evidence."

At this, Wadsworth made a completely irrelevant statement in order to divert the judge and the matter was permitted to slip by.

As we left the courthouse I told Paul I wanted a copy of the transcript immediately. This information was going to be vital to the hearings in California because it would contradict Mark's own testimony in the Van Nuys deposition.

Within a couple of days I had in my hand a copy of a letter Paul sent to Robert Lewis confirming his phone call requesting a transcript as quickly as possible. Weeks went by and nothing happened. I called Paul and reminded him of the importance of this matter. Again he wrote to Lewis. Months passed this time. Finally, I called Lewis myself and told him how important the document was to the hearing scheduled for November 19th. He told me he would get right on it.

On November 15th, almost four months after the hearing, I called again. Mr. Lewis was out, but I left word. The next day a girl called. Mr. Lewis said that the transcripts would be ready Monday morning; however, I was to call before I came by to pick them up, and it would be necessary to have a check for the amount of the transcribing.

This delay meant that it would be past the time I would be able to use the transcript in the hearing in L.A. As a last resort, I made a reservation on a mid-morning flight out of Salt Lake City on Monday, thinking I would pick up the transcript before I left. I called as they had asked and Mr. Lewis said he thought it was almost ready but copies would have to be made and I couldn't pick them up until the following day. I wondered what kind of a game was being conducted in an office dealing with official court records.

On Tuesday morning, November 20th, I picked up the delayed copies, went back to my office and read the whole transcript carefully, word by word. When I came to page 83, line 22, I read: "It varies. I give my wife $1,000.00 every month to take care of the house payment and bills."

I read it over several times. I couldn't believe my eyes, but there it was: *$1,000.00!* I tried to call Paul but he wasn't in. For the next four days I tried to contact Paul at three-hour intervals. Finally I learned that he was out for Thanksgiving weekend.

Discouraged, I went home and asked Louise what Mark had answered when the judge asked about his income. With no hesitation she answered, "$3,000.00." Without prodding for the answer, I asked several others who attended the trial. Each of them answered, "$3,000.00."

I started to study the transcript. The typing of the figures $1000.00 seemed conspicuously darker than any of the other letters or figures on the page. Mine was a copy, so the original would have been even darker. I looked again. There was a slight line above the one in the figure and in examining more closely, I saw that the $1,000.00 figure was not on a perfect line with the rest of the typing.

I couldn't wait for Paul. On Friday I called another attorney and asked what I should do. He thought I should call Mr. Lewis first and tell him that I thought there was an error in the transcript. Everyone was out for Thanksgiving. I couldn't reach Lewis either.

But on Monday morning I made contact with him. I asked if he still had the transcript he had taken at the time of the hearing. He asked why. I told him I thought there might have been an error made and I wanted him to check on it. A stony silence followed. Finally he tried to assure me that they had proof-read the transcript and it was correct. There was no need to check it with the original transcript. Besides, it would take some time to do something like that.

I decided it was time to get tough. I informed him that I was so upset when I read the transcript that I took it to eight others who were in the courtroom and without any prompting, they all answered as I suspected they would. I told him about the error and said that all eight of the witnesses were willing to come down and sign affidavits to that effect.

He said nothing for a minute, so I went on. I would proceed to get the affidavits and file for a court order to preserve the original form of the manuscript. He acted like a little kid caught with his hand in the cookie jar. "By the way," I asked, "did Mr. Wadsworth or Mr. Young speak to you about the amount on the transcript?" I was getting more suspicious by the minute. "Absolutely not!" he sputtered. "I will review the transcript and get back to you."

I told him I would be happy to wait. "No," he said, "it will take longer than that." I tried to pin him down. "How long?" I asked. He answered about forty-five minutes.

But about ten minutes later he called me back. "Mr.

Mann, you are right. There was an error made in the amount. It was $3,000.00. I have talked to Judge Baldwin and he said it is not necessary to do it over again, just to make a notation on it. I will do this and have it changed so that the copy at the clerk's office reads $3,000.00."

I told him I wanted a notarized letter sent to me to that effect, that an error had been made and the correct figure was $3,000.00. Reluctantly, he agreed to do this. On November 28th I received the following letter:

THIRD JUDICIAL DISTRICT COURT
ROBERT F. LEWIS, C.S.R.
Official Court Reporter
Salt Lake City, Utah 84111
Nov. 26, 1979

PAUL H. LIAPIS
Attorney at Law
1000 Boston Bldg.
Salt Lake City, Utah 84111
RE: In the matter of: DAVID MARK NEWTON WHEELER, a minor, Case No. P-79-2

Dear Paul:

I received a call from your client, Stan Mann, today, He suggested that I might have made an error in the Transcript of Proceedings dated July 23, 1979, heard before the Honorable Ernest F. Baldwin, Jr., Judge.

This letter is to inform you that upon checking my stenographic notes, I do find an error on page 83 line 22. Page 83 line 22 now reads: "A. It varies. I give my wife *$1000.00* a month every month". It should read: "A. It varies. I give my wife *$3000.00* a month every month".

I have inerliniated the correction on the original transcript—which has been filed in the Salt Lake County Clerk's

Office—and initialed and dated the page and line.

Please accept my apology for any inconvenience this may have caused you or your client. If you have any questions, please feel free to call me.

        Sincerely,

        ROBERT F. LEWIS, C.S.R.

cc   Court file
      Stan Mann

My mind was running rampant. Aware of other tactics Wadsworth and Young had used as officers of the law, I determined to go down to the courthouse and check the transcript myself. I postponed a trip to San Francisco in order to follow through on this.

On Friday, the 30th, at the clerk's office I found a copy of Lewis' letter, and in examining the original transcript, I found exactly what I had expected. The $1,000.00 had been written on top of correction fluid! At the top of the "1" there was a slight curve resembling the top of the figure "3"—obviously omitted from the fluid. I was convinced that the original figure had read $3,000.00, and Mr. Lewis' behavior simply confirmed my opinion that either Wadsworth or Young had taken it upon themselves to have the figure changed.

Unbelievable in a democracy? Once I would have said as much. Now I know better. When I observe the actions of these two attorneys, I find it impossible to believe that all of these things happened merely by chance. And later I learned that Paul Liapis never received a copy of that letter. In fact, he was not even aware of what had happened!

In a hearing held before the Colorado Division of Labor, Mark Wheeler was awarded $752.26 per month support money for David by the Division of Labor and Social Security, on the basis of Joan's employment. When Joan was alive, she could not collect a third of that amount monthly from Mark for the boy's support—although the courts had awarded it to her. The moral: abandon your wife and child, and if you are lucky, you won't have to pay any support money. Furthermore, if she dies, you can collect three times more per month than she had coming. And all of this will be legal and above board. Justice? Equality?

In Denver, Mark made several comments to Loren Yeates, the lawyer who represented Joan's estate. Loren was so completely taken in with Mark that he called me to say that I had him all wrong. Mark wanted to have good relations with us. He thought David needed family ties. Loren was convinced that Mark had the boy's best interests at heart. I wished with all my heart that he was right, but I knew Mark too well.

Still, I wasn't prepared for what happened on Saturday, December 29th. I picked up an Ogden paper as we were leaving town for a three-day vacation, and there, staring at me in bold type was a headline of an article: MAN CLAIMS COUPLE TRIED TO HAVE HIM KILLED; SUES. I read on, frantically.

Ogden Standard Examiner 12-29-79

Man Claims Couple Tried To Have Him Killed; Sues

SALT LAKE CITY (UPI)—A California man Friday filed a $616,000 federal court suit against a Salt Lake City couple, claiming they attempted to prevent him from gaining custody of his adopted son, and then tried to have him killed.

Mark W. Wheeler of Northridge, Calif., filed the suit before Judge David Winder of the U.S. District Court for Utah. He named Stanley C. Mann and his wife Louise Mann as defendants.

Wheeler said he and his first wife, Joan, adopted their son, David, after they had attempted unsuccessfully for 10 years to have children of their own. The Wheelers divorced in 1976. His wife was granted custody of the son and Wheeler given visitation rights.

Joan Wheeler was killed Dec. 28, 1978, in the crash of a United Airlines jet in Oregon. The woman had left her adopted son in the care of her aunt and uncle—the Manns.

In his lawsuit, Wheeler claims he called the Manns to determine the whereabouts of David, but the Manns told him the boy "is not your concern any more and you will never see him again."

Wheeler sued in state court in Utah to be named the child's custodian. But he said the Manns also filed suit to be declared David's legal guardians. The father claims the only way the uncle and aunt could be named guardians was for him to be declared incompetent or deceased.

Wheeler claims the Manns "conspired" to have him killed, and he was attacked by a gunman outside his Southern California home.

Wheeler is seeking $400,000 in punitive damages from the Manns, $160,000 in general damages, $27,000 to reimburse him for lost income while he recovered from his gunshot wounds, $20,000 in medical expenses, and $8,904 for attorneys fees.

Friends started calling us. This article appeared in all the local papers and on television as well. What a jolt. This was the first we had heard of anything like this. What a way to establish good relations with us! The whole thing was incredible. I was being sued for trying to carry out responsibilities delegated to me under terms of a will, and then accused of conspiracy to murder. My mind was spinning, but I knew what had to be done.

On January 10, 1980, I hired Gordon L. Roberts to represent me regarding these accusations, and he immediately served summons on Mark's brother-in-law, Wayne Wadsworth, for depositions to be taken on Sylvi and Mark. They would have received these notices no later than January 21st, requesting their presence in Salt Lake City on Thursday, January 31st and Friday, February 1st.

By January 24th, I was preparing to leave for Denver for the hearing regarding Mark's motion to have Joan's will thrown out as well as to hear charges that I was in contempt of court. Wadsworth claimed that papers had been served on me to appear at his office for a deposition. I had not heard anything about this, nor had my attorney, and Paul Liapis had supplied the Denver attorney with an affidavit to that effect.

I was greatly concerned about Louise's health. She was suffering from unusual abdominal pains which the doctors couldn't seem to diagnose, and her blood pressure had skyrocketed. She had reason to feel ill. Rumors had come to us that the news had spread to Chicago and New Jersey where we formerly lived. Her gentle disposition could not cope with everything that had been thrown at us.

I decided to delay my departure to the airport as late as possible, then I made up my mind that I would not go to Denver at all. I took her to the doctor's and the tests that he administered, trying to locate the source of her problems, took all morning. I called the attorney in Denver, of course, and informed him of the situation.

When I returned to my office at noon, I found a message to call Loren Yeates in Denver. At long last: good news! Loren informed me that the court had handed down the decision that Mark Wheeler had no standing. The judge ruled that his attorneys had no legal right to depose me regarding the estate or the will, and consequently Wadsworth's attempts to have me cited for contempt of court had failed.

On the same day as the Denver hearing, later in the afternoon, Gordon Roberts called Wadsworth relative to Mark's and Sylvi's depositions. Wadsworth insisted it would not be possible to hold these depositions on the 31st and the 1st, inasmuch as Mark would be out of the country. He had to make a business trip to South Africa, an employment opportunity that would keep him out of the country until somewhere around the middle of March. Roberts said he would not agree to this kind of postponement. They would have to have a hearing before a judge.

Mark had never mentioned this trip while he was in Denver. Roberts informed Wadsworth that he knew Mark was in Denver and he could give his deposition in Salt Lake City on his way back to California. Wadsworth said that was not possible. There was a hearing on this matter on January 29th before Judge David K. Winder in the United States District Court for the State of Utah.

Wadsworth had everything planned. He presented Judge Winder with a letter from Mark with the instructions that the letter was for the judge's eyes only. Mr. Wheeler, he said, was concerned about his life because of me, and only the judge could read his letter. Check this situation: Wadsworth was upset when I didn't appear at the hearing in Denver. Mark had been in Denver where he expected to see me and yet he wasn't concerned about his life then. Mark had also been in Utah and Idaho—where I was at large—and he wasn't concerned about his life. But now, suddenly, he was afraid!

After reading the letter, Judge Winder asked, "Is this Mr. Wheeler an accountant for Touche Ross?" Wadsworth, after a hesitation and a bit of stammering, said, "Well, no, Your Honor. He is sort of...a...ah...ah...in business...ah...management." He was visably shaken. He hadn't expected the judge to mention Touche Ross. Wadsworth's stammering made me doubt the authenticity of that letter. Perhaps the Judge had reservations, too. At any rate, he granted the continuance on the condition that they both appear on March 12th and 13th for the depositions.

Back at my office, I called my attorney in California and asked him to check with Touche Ross. In less than one hour he called back to report that Touche Ross said Mark's employment with them ended in 1976 and he had not worked for them since.

I wondered what kind of game Wadsworth was playing. Mark is only concerned for his life when he has need for secrecy. Is Wadsworth setting the scene for something to happen to Mark so he can point the finger of guilt at me? Is this why he seems to be laying the groundwork for David to be given to Sylvi, in the event of a divorce—or in case something happens to Mark?

If he can frame me, then Sylvi would not only continue to get over $9,000.00 a year from the Department of Labor because of Joan's death, but in addition she might stand a good chance of getting control of David's trust.

As I look back, it seems that anytime Mark extended a tiny gesture toward conciliation, Wadsworth went out of his way to promote dissension. Paul Liapis once made the observation that Wadsworth would keep up his legal harassment of me until they got their hands on the money. He could think of no other reason, after the offers we had made to them on the condition that they not try to break Joan's trust.

Wadsworth is aware that Mark has several judgments against him, that his former friend, Jim Coleman (from whom Mark borrowed money which he lost in an investment and never repaid) was indicted for land fraud. Wadsworth also knows, from Mark's own admission, that he purchased a hand gun under a false name and with false identification in Arizona, and surely he is aware of Mark's extra-marital activities and Joan's statements that Mark threatened her life. Maybe Wadsworth is trying to protect his sister-in-law—and his fee. (One judge turned down Wadsworth's request for payment of his fee, but he is trying to collect through another court.)

Yes, I guess Wadsworth is probably right: Mark Wheeler has reason to fear for his life. After all, someone *did* try to kill him—and it wasn't me. But maybe I'll be next. Obviously from Wadsworth's conspiring, I have cause to be fearful, too. There is no doubt in my mind that Wadsworth and Dave Young have conspired to libel and slander me. Recent records from Wadsworth's own office reveal that they plotted together to have Dave and Shauna go to one of the Church's General Authorities under the guise of asking his counsel. They used this opportunity to try to discredit me,—and then they had the nerve to charge legal fees for this consultation!

Recently, license plates were stolen from my car and with everything else that has happened to me and my family—threatening phone calls, cutting our security wires, constant legal harassment, accusations of intent to commit murder... well, someone is trying to do harm to me. How far they'll go, I don't know.

But again, I am determined to continue the fight.

I want to feel—I *need* to feel—that America is still a land of justice and equality. And that just because someone is dead—or a child—his rights will not be obliterated by the acts and connivings of unscrupulous men. I am impelled to push this case. Someone has to speak up, or all of us—and our country—are doomed. Maybe my job is to be that spokesman.

Afterword

To my surprise Mark and Sylvi appeared for their depositions on March 12th and 13th, 1980, as ordered by Judge Winder. The words they uttered under oath merely confirmed my feelings about the conspiracy against me, and I was beginning to realize that Mark had played only a minor role. It was Sylvi and Wadsworth's show.

I was certain, but now the courts had to be convinced, and I learned that the wheels of justice move with agonizing slowness. After the depositions were taken, I had to wait three long weeks to secure official transcripts, and then my attorney and I had to consider every alternative action and reach some hard decisions.

Meanwhile, Louise and I were under accusation of conspiracy to murder, and that is a mighty uncomfortable position for a couple who have always prided themselves on being honest, straight-forward American citizens. Adding to my discomfort were the rumors I heard that both the Youngs and Wadsworth were assassinating our character in—of all places—church meetings, social events and other gatherings where such matters should never be discussed. I was shocked. That kind of behavior never fails to disturb me, especially when it emanates from "good, Christian" folks.

Roberts and I finally arrived at a course of action. We would ask for complete dismissal for Louise. They didn't have a shred of evidence against her, and our attorney thought dismissal would come readily in view of their blatantly chauvinistic charges. Their only "evidence" was that she was my wife and secretary!

It was a little different story for me. I had affadavits from half a dozen people, placing me over 800 miles away from Los Angeles on the night Mark was shot, but under hypnosis Sylvi claimed to have seen me at the scene of the crime. Mark made no such claims. The more I thought about it, the more I felt Sylvi and Wadsworth were in collusion in this nasty business, and that Mark was an "also-ran." Sylvi was convinced of my guilt long before she was ever put under hypnosis. How important are one's own wishes in determining what one "sees" under hypnosis, I wondered?

Apparently the police did not believe her, for I was never arrested. Every time she opened her mouth, her stories varied, and I was inclined to think that pathological liars are attracted to each other.

Under hypnosis she said that she saw me coming out of the shadows between two buildings approximately 70 feet away. In her deposition, she said she was near her front door and locked eyes with me while I was standing on a mound of dirt under a street light approximately 150 feet away. In actuality the closest street light adjacent to her home is 245 feet from her property line. Physical facilities defy her story. The shooting took place at 10:30 at night. Imagine locking eyes at a distance of 150 feet at night where there is no light!

I later contacted Detective Ritter on the telephone. He confirmed that I was a suspect merely because Mark and Sylvi said so. "There was certainly no evidence that we could dig up that showed you had anything to do with it."

In spite of the fact that the opposition had no "hard" evidence against me, I wanted to see the case through. My attorney said it was important to clear my name. He could not ask for dismissal for me because dismissals are granted only when there is "no disputation of fact" and Sylvi's claim—flimsy as it was—ruled that out. Most states, Roberts told me, do not admit evidence induced under hypnosis, but Utah has not ruled one way or the other.

On May 21st, we met in Judge Winder's courtroom. Only a few people were present: Louise and I, of course, and our attorneys; Wadsworth, my sisters Alice and Frances for moral support; a couple of our friends, and a reporter or two. They didn't bother me; I had nothing to hide. I wanted the whole matter aired.

Judge Winder started the proceedings by stating that he could see no evidence that indicated Louise had any part in any conspiracy to commit murder. He wondered if Wadsworth had any additional information on this subject. Wadsworth had nothing new to offer. He insisted that Louise must be part of the conspiracy because she was my wife and my personal secretary. She had been in on taped phone calls and stood to gain financially in the custody suit if Mark were killed. The Manns, Wadsworth repeated, were the only persons with motive to kill Mark, and he was certain that Louise was part of that conspiracy.

His main argument against Louise was that, in his opinion, she lied about my whereabouts on the night of the shooting. Both the Judge and Roberts denied him the basis for such reasoning, and when Wadsworth mentioned the custody suit, Judge Winder commended that it was indeed "a giant step" from a custody case to conspiracy to murder. "I'll hear you out," he told Wadsworth, "but we need facts."

He had no facts. Again he tried to bluff, but Judge Winder

caught him by noting that certainly we could not incriminate a woman simply because she happens to be married to a man accused of a crime, or because she is his secretary. Wadsworth mumbled something about further discovery, but Roberts said there had been ample time for further discovery if they were going to pursue that course of action. Furthermore, when Wadsworth kept insisting that we were the only ones with motive to kill Mark, Roberts stated emphatically that we were not responsible for finding the perpetrator of the crime.

Wadsworth had recently asked to withdraw from the case, giving non-payment of fees as his reason. We had expected this, but not at this point. We figured they intended to blacken our name but not actually go to court. Wadsworth wanted us to believe that the Wheeler's were paying their lawyers in California and Colorado, but were not paying their brother-in-law in Utah. They picked the wrong time to withdraw. Obviously we had a judge who could see through their game. Wadsworth was playing in the big league now. Neither Judge Winder nor my attorneys were bamboozled by his tactics, and even though he clung tenaciously to his story, something was different about him. He acted—how shall I put it?—as if the wind had been knocked out of him, like a little boy whose hands had been slapped (by the other members of his law firm, perhaps?) He was subdued, to put it mildly. If his previous behavior hadn't been so dastardly, I might have felt sorry for him. Ray Etcheverry said "I have never seen another lawyer fumble so badly trying to cover his ass".

Wadsworth shot his last wad. He said he had great difficulty in deposing us. Actually we had been ready to leave for his office to give depositions the previous Friday when we were notified not to come as he was withdrawing from the case. Obviously his plan was to withdraw so our depositions and the affidavits verifying my whereabouts the night of the shooting could not be entered into evidence and made available to the court.

Wadsworth's last attempts were half-hearted and futile. Judge Winder granted a summary judgement and dismissed the case against Louise. We both drew a deep breath. Finally, things were looking a little brighter. We wanted to go home, to feel a sense of freedom, and to be able to enjoy our family without having to peer over our shoulders constantly.

But Roberts wasn't through. He asked the judge for a speedy trial so that the matter could be cleared up in short order. The judge respected our situation but because of scheduling problems, he would have to stick to the September 21st trial date. However, and he emphasized this point, Wadsworth's withdrawl from the case would in no way cause prolongation or postponement of the trial except in the most serious of conditions such as death. He warned Wadsworth that counsel must be obtained or he would be forced to return to the case—or in the event that this was not possible, Mark and Sylvi would have to defend their own charges!

These were the only conditions under which Judge Winder would accept Wadsworth's withdrawl from the case. Louise and I exchanged looks. Finally we had found an intelligent judge. It was almost too good to be true, after all of our disillusionment. Now it seemed that I would receive a fair trial. That's what we had wanted all along: a chance for our day in court.

I wanted this case aired more than ever. Now they were starting to bargain. Only the week before the hearing, they offered to settle out of court if I would agree to a polygraph test. Hell, that wouldn't bother me. I had offered to take a lie detector test way back in September, but they weren't interested. Now I wasn't. Roberts advised me to turn them down. We stood to gain more by going to trial.

My step was lighter than it had been in months when we left the courtroom. I wasn't out of the woods yet, not by any means, but with a rational jury and a fair judge, I would have a chance to unravel this whole mess. On the way back to the office, I told Louise that within a week to ten days they would approach us with an offer to avoid going to trial. I was wrong. Within *three hours* our lawyer was on the phone. They had already approached him! It was amazing that Wadsworth, who had withdrawn, was now trying to negotiate with me. I refused to deal with him and related to my attorney that we would deal only with the Wheelers or their new counsel, and then only relative to the damages against Louise. As for my situation, I would not negotiate with anyone. I insisted on going to trial so that everything would be brought out in the open.

Something had to be done. It was evident to me that an unethical lawyer, empowered with legal knowledge and as an officer of the court, was more dangerous practicing law than a strangler running loose in the city with diplomatic immunity, without a police force to subdue his actions. We had to get everything out in the open. A trial by jury was the only way.

If we could untangle this web of deception, maybe somehow, God willing, we could find justice for little David, too.

As I examine this whole situation with the added advantage of distance brought on by the passing of time, I still feel that the devastation wrought upon my family by these circumstances is appalling. My wife, my children and I have all been subjected to unbelievable tension and embarrassment. Imagine having your daughter's date call for her and someone remarking to the youth, "You'd better treat her right, or her father will send his gunman after you!" Even in fun, this statement hurts. My wife's health failed to the point that I feared for her survival, and if I had not had—or found—the $30,000 required to fight these unwarranted charges, if I hadn't been in a position to handle all these legal matters, I shudder to think what would have happened to my family. What if I had not owned my own business? If I had been employed by someone else, I would surely have lost my means of livelihood. And even more important, if my family hadn't been made of sturdy stock, we might have broken under the strain.

The ramifications of a situation like this are horrifying. Instead of concerning ourselves to such a marked degree with the rights of alleged criminals, we should look to the rights of the victims of crime. Our state and national legislators should enact laws to protect and compensate these victims in direct proportion to protection provided for the guilty. We *must* find ways to put a stop to legal harrassment and brutality!

After the original writing of this book was completed, a number of things transpired which lent further credence to my stand. Wayne Wadsworth's resignation opened the way for Mark to retain a young lawyer named Steve Trost.

Trost was represented as independent, but we soon learned that he shared offices with Dave Young and his name was imprinted on the door to that office as a member of Dave's firm. Apparently he worked right along with Young, just as Wadsworth had.

The case against Louise was dismissed, of course, and when the judge denied a postponement in the trial scheduled for September 21st against me, they submitted a false affidavit stating their inability to depose Detective Ritter until the latter part of October because he had undergone open heart surgery. We made a telephone call and found that Ritter was well enough to give a deposition at any time and that he had returned to work, full-time, by the first part of August.

Trost soon made a motion to dismiss the conspiracy to commit murder charges against me with prejudice, which means they could never bring the same charges again, and the charges were indeed dropped. But note this: He had never taken a single deposition or made any attempts at discovery from the onset of the charges! And neither had Wadsworth, until Trost deposed Lt. Gaida and immediately moved for dismissal of all charges.

I shortly received a subpoena to appear in court to show cause why I shouldn't be held in contempt. Documents indicated that I had failed to comply with court orders. I hadn't received any court orders! I represented myself at this hearing, and the judge's findings proved that all documents had been sent to an improper address. I also learned that I had been removed as trustee of David's trust on the basis of erroneous information supplied by Mr. Trost. All charges against me were dismissed and the previous order by the judge to remove me as trustee was vacated.

These same erroneous documents were used in California (even though the judge had vacated the order) to postpone the hearing on the closing of Joan's estate. Postponement was granted until September 29th at which time neither Mark not his attorney showed up. The judge ordered the estate to be disbursed as we had requested.

It seemed that my adversaries had intentionally plotted to frame me, to disturb and threaten me to the point of violence, but then when they reached the stage of having to put up or shut up, they made a motion to dismiss their own charges against me. Under British justice we would have been awarded court costs, legal fees and damages, but because of the conspiracy of the American legal profession to create situations where people are forced to use their services, we must put out additional thousands of dollars to recoup these expenses and damages. All of this unnecessary litigation is bogging down our courts and legal system.

Wayne Wadsworth and his client were told by the L.A. police that there was absolutely no evidence linking me to the shooting of Mark Wheeler in any way. They knew this, and yet they filed a suit against me—with NO EVIDENCE. My family and I suffered under these charges for almost eight months before they were finally dismissed, *with prejudice*, from a motion made by the very people who brought them against us in the first place! They admitted under oath that they had no information that the L.A. Police Department did not have, and still they filed their suit.

I was raised to respect and honor the American flag and the American system, and it is difficult for me to cast aspersions against anything connected with the American way. Yet, from my own personal experiences—which often seemed like a nightmare, rather than something happening to me right here in my own beloved country—I know that we must analyze and remedy legal procedures traditional to our time. Sometimes at night I still awaken in a cold sweat when I realize what might have happened to me.

God willing, my story may help to open some eyes that need to be opened, to provide some insight into the problem so that conscientious citizens and legislators alike will assume responsibility in correcting these evils. This country has too much going for it to let a group of unscrupulous professionals polute its entire future.

Mentally I write my niece one last message:

Joan, dear,

It was a real hornet's nest we stirred up here in Zion, but these problems exist and they need to be uncovered.

Things are looking better now, and Uncle Stan's going to do his best by you. The court decisions are finally going our way, and I am making a concentrated effort to find David's real parents. We may yet provide for that little fellow. It looks as if the storm is blowing over.

The time may come when we will not have to face any more harrassing law suits.

I pray Aunt Louise will soon feel like her old self, and our home will once again be a haven of peace, just as you remembered it.

But whatever comes, Joan, rest assured that I'll never let them have David's money, and if God grants me enough days and sufficient means, before I die, I'll see that boy in a home with loving parents.

This I promise you, niece of mine. Be at peace. We love you.

Uncle Stan

References

Complaint dated November 28, 1975, Complaint 234178, Civil 21241. Plaintiff—Charles William Newton Vs Defendant—Shauna N. Young. District Court of Davis County, Utah. Later moved to Salt Lake County by David Young.

2nd Codicil to the will of Charles W. Newton, dated 2nd August, 1975.

Abstract of Judgment. Superior Court of California, County of Los Angeles. Joan N. Wheeler, Plaintiff Vs Mark Wayne Wheeler. December 18, 1978.

Examination of Judgment. Debtor Mark Wayne Wheeler, Van Nuys, California. March 1, 1979. Estate of Joan N. Wheeler Vs Mark Wayne Wheeler NWD 58814.

Decree of Adoption # AD 89908. Superior Court of California, County of Los Angeles. December 19, 1975.

Divorce Case # NWD 58814. Superior Court of California, County of Los Angeles. Joan N. Wheeler, Petitioner Vs Mark Wayne Wheeler, Respondent. January 7, 1976.

Deposition of Joan Wheeler. San Diego, California, August 21, 1976. Joan N. Wheeler Vs Mark Wayne Wheeler NWD 58814.

Deposition of Mark Wayne Wheeler, San Diego, California, August 21, 1976. Joan N. Wheeler Vs Mark Wayne Wheeler NWD 58814.

Deposition of Mark Wayne Wheeler. Salt Lake City, Utah. June 20, 1979. Matter, David Mark Newton Wheeler, A Minor, Probate P-79-2.

Deposition of Sylvi Wheeler, Beverly Hills, California. October 10, 1977. Dick Robinson.Vs Mel Hardman Productions. #218709 (Civil).

Deposition, Raylan Jensen, Salt Lake City. November 29, 1976 & April 14, 1977. Dick Robinson Vs Mel Hardman Productions. Civil 218709.

Deposition of Robert H. Marshall, M.D. Encino, California. June 28, 1979. Matter, David Mark Newton Wheeler, A Minor. P-79-2.

Deposition of William Richard Treu, Encino, California. June 28, 1979. Matter, David Mark Newton Wheeler, A Minor. P-79-2.

Deposition of Norma Ann Waldman, Encino, California. June 28, 1979. Matter, David Mark Newton Wheeler, A Minor. P-79-2.

Deposition of Keith R. Haight, Encino, California. June 28, 1979. Matter, David Mark Newton Wheeler, A Minor. P-79-2.

Petition to Terminate Order of Temporary Guardianship. Salt Lake City, Utah. January 12, 1979. Matter, David Mark Newton Wheeler, A Minor. P-79-2. Judge: Bryant Croft.

Petition to Terminate Guardianship and Order that Minor Be Delivered to Father. Salt Lake City, Utah. January 4, 1979. Matter, David Mark Newton Wheeler, A Minor P-79-2. Judge: Bryant Croft.

Transcript of Proceedings in the Matter of David Mark Wheeler. July 23, 1979. Third District Court, Salt Lake County, Utah.

National Transportation Safety Board Report #NTSB-AAR—79-7. June 7, 1979. Titled, Aircraft Accident Report—United Airlines Inc. McDonnel-Douglas DC-8-61, N 8082U. Portland, Oregon. December 28, 1978.

Personal History of Joan Newton Wheeler. 1942-1978

Diary, Notes, Letters, and Tapes by/to Joan Newton Wheeler. 1966-1978.

Letters, Tapes, and Notes by Mark Wayne Wheeler. 1966-1975.

Letters from Wayne Wadsworth to Paul Liapis and Byron Fisher.

Deposition of Mark Wayne Wheeler, Salt Lake City, Utah, March 12, 1980 in matter of Mark and Sylvi Wheeler Vs Stanley and Louise Mann. Civil #C-79-0772 W.

Deposition of Sylvi Wheeler, Salt Lake City, Utah, March 13, 1980 in the matter of Mark and Sylvi Wheeler Vs Stanley and Louise Mann. Civil #C-79-0772 W.

Transcript of motion for summary judgement on Louise S. Mann. U.S. District Court of Utah. Civil #C-79-0772 W. May 21, 1980.

Transcript of motion to withdraw as counsel for the plaintiffs by Wayne Wadsworth. U.S. District Court of Utah. Civil #C-79-0772 W. May 21, 1980.

Affidavit of Stephen A. Trost #C-79-0772 W. U.S. District Court of Utah. July 7, 1980.

Letter to The Honorable David K. Winder. United States District Court Judge. July 14, 1980. Raymond J. Etcheverry. #C-79-0772 W.

Order of Dismissal with Prejudice. Mark W. Wheeler and Sylvi Wheeler Vs Stanley C. Mann and Louise S. Mann. U.S. District Court of Utah. #C-79-0772 W. July 18, 1980.

Plaintiffs Order to Show Cause. Third Judicial District Court. Salt Lake County. August 29, 1980. #C-79-4063.